BRAZIL

AN INTERPRETATION

BY

GILBERTO FREYRE

NEW YORK : ALFRED A. KNOPF

1945

CONTENTS

PREFACE ... v

I. THE EUROPEAN BACKGROUND OF BRAZILIAN HISTORY ... 1

II. FRONTIER AND PLANTATION IN BRAZIL ... 35

III. BRAZILIAN UNITY AND BRAZILIAN REGIONAL DIVERSITY ... 66

IV. ETHNIC AND SOCIAL CONDITIONS IN MODERN BRAZIL ... 91

V. BRAZILIAN FOREIGN POLICY AS CONDITIONED BY BRAZIL'S ETHNIC, CULTURAL, AND GEOGRAPHICAL SITUATION ... 123

VI. THE MODERN LITERATURE OF BRAZIL: ITS RELATION TO BRAZILIAN SOCIAL PROBLEMS ... 155

INDEX ... *follows page* 179

✦ PREFACE ✦

These lectures were delivered on the Patten Foundation at Indiana University during the autumn of 1944.

As in my previous essays and lectures on the social history of Brazil, published in Portuguese, Spanish, and English, the point of view is that of one who attempts to suggest a philosophy of Brazilian ethnic and social "fusionism," not the point of view of rigidly impartial historians or sociologists, if such historians and sociologists really exist.

As a work of interpretation or synthesis, prepared especially for an Anglo-American public, these lectures are based on the various monographs that the author has written on the subject. In these monographs, particularly in Casa Grande & Senzala, *published in Portuguese and Spanish and soon forthcoming in English, the reader will find a more detailed presentation of a number of the topics here discussed and also fuller bibliographies.*

I thank the authorities of Indiana University for their invitation to me to be the Patten Lecturer for 1944. I shall long remember the courtesies received from President Herman B Wells, from the trustees, members of the faculty, and students, and especially from Professors Cleland, Mueller, Rey, Laurent, Tomašič, Winther, and Engel. In particular, I should like to mention how much I was helped in the preparation of the manuscript of these lectures for the press by my friend Professor Laurens J. Mills of the English Department. Many thanks are due also to Miss Ruth Anderson for her patient work as a typist.

G. F.

Bloomington

BRAZIL
AN INTERPRETATION

I

THE EUROPEAN BACKGROUND OF BRAZILIAN HISTORY

BRAZIL, which was discovered and colonized by the Portuguese, is sometimes called Portuguese America. As Portuguese America it is generally considered an extension of Europe, and in its main characteristics it remains Portuguese and Hispanic, or Iberian. It is also Catholic, or a branch or variant of the Latin form of Christianity or civilization.

But the facts that its origins are mainly Portuguese or Hispanic and that its principal characteristics are Latin Catholic do not make of Brazil so simple or pure an extension of Europe as New England was of old England and as New England was of Protestant or Evangelical Christianity in North America. For, as everyone knows, Spain and Portugal, though conventionally European states, are not orthodox in all their European and Christian qualities, experiences, and conditions of life, but are in many important respects a mixture of Europe and Africa, of Christianity and Mohammedanism. According to geographers the Hispanic peninsula is a transition zone between two continents; it is a popular saying that "Africa begins in the Pyrenees" —a saying sometimes used sarcastically by Nordics.

For eight centuries the Hispanic, or Iberian, peninsula was dominated by Africans. Arabs and Moors left their trace there. Though some of the modern Spanish and Portuguese thinkers (like Unamuno) would have Spain and Portugal Europeanized with all speed, others (like Ganivet) maintain that Spain and Portugal must look south, to Africa, for their future and for the explanation of their ethos. The same conflict of opinion is to be found among foreign students of Hispanic social history and cultural problems: some—the German, Schulten, for instance—believe that one of the tasks of modern Europe should be to definitely annex Spain to the European system of civilization; while others—the Frenchman, Maurice Legendre, for instance—go so far as to say that the African element is one of the best original ingredients of Spain, not to be repudiated with shame but to be cherished with pride.

Legendre is one of the authors who point out the similarity between the Spanish peninsula and Russia in their being each a transition zone between two continents: "*Elle* [Spain, or Iberia] *est à la rencontre de deux continents comme la Russie.*" [1] And not only between two continents, one might add: between two climates, two types of soil and vegetation, two races, two cultures, two conceptions of life, two ecological complexes

---

1. Maurice Legendre, *Portrait de l'Espagne* (Paris, 1923), p. 49. The situation of the Hispanic peninsula as a transition zone is certainly similar in many important respects to that of Russia, described by Professor Hans Kohn as "a meeting place of the East and the West by her history and by her nature" (*Orient and Occident*, New York, 1934, p. 76).

The European Background 3

—and between Euro-Africa and Hispanic America.

As in Russia, such antagonistic conditions and conceptions of life as are to be found among Spaniards and Portuguese have not come together without violent conflict. But amalgamation, accommodation, assimilation have been more powerful than conflict. The result is that the Portuguese, like the Spanish and the Russians, are, in more than a cultural and social aspect, a people with the "split" or Dr. Jekyll-Mr. Hyde personality that psychologists have studied in certain individuals, and that sociologists have perceived in certain social groups. In other aspects, however, they are made not only more dramatic but psychologically richer and culturally more complex than simpler peoples by the fact that they have developed a special capacity to maintain contradictions and even to harmonize them. This capacity is now being demonstrated impressively by the Russians; and it has been demonstrated by the Spanish and the Portuguese during the most creative phases of their history, through one or another of the classical methods by which individuals and groups solve their inner conflicts of personality. According to modern American sociologists and social psychologists such solutions are, fundamentally, three: (1) the rejection of one element or interest, usually by repression, and the selection of another, opposing one; (2) the splitting of the personality into two or more divisions, each looking toward some interest or objects; (3) integration, or balance, of contending elements.

If I am not mistaken, each of the three classical solutions could be found as a dominant factor in any of the various phases of the social and cultural development of the Spanish and Portuguese peoples. Of these phases, that which concerns us most directly is the one that immediately preceded the discovery of the American continent and the colonization of it by Spanish and Portuguese. But the truth is that the social and psychological preparation—unconscious preparation—of the Spaniards and the Portuguese for that tremendous task seems to have taken the entire eight centuries of close contact of the Spanish and Portuguese Christians with the Arabs and Moors who dominated the peninsula. For such centuries were not all, or only, centuries of war, conflict, intolerance. As Professor Fernando de los Ríos reminds us, there were epochs of struggle and intolerance but also "marvelous periods of understanding and co-operation." "To stress the latter we have only to remember," he writes, "how in the thirteenth century the three cults—Christian, Moorish and Mosaic —were celebrated in the same temple, the mosque of Santa María la Blanca de Toledo." [2]

On the other hand, the periods of Castilian and orthodox Catholic domination over the so-called "Hispanic totality" seem to illustrate the solution—or attempt at a solution—of co-existent ethnic and cultural antagonisms through rejecting or repressing various elements and selecting one stock or group and one culture or religion as the perfect or orthodox one: the Inquisi-

---

2. "Spain in the Epoch of American Civilization," in *Concerning Latin American Culture* (New York, 1940), p. 24.

The European Background 5

tion was perhaps the most powerful instrument used in Spain and Portugal to accomplish this end. But neither Castilian centralization nor the Inquisition was able to repress differences or entirely neutralize the process of accommodation in the cultural field and the process of amalgamation in the biological and ethnic one. The *mozarabes* (Christians living under Mohammedan rule), the *mudejares* (Moors living under Christian rule), and the *New Christians* (Jews completely or superficially converted to Christianity) had in Spain and Portugal become too powerful, too penetrating, too plastic, too fluid, and too complex to allow Spanish or Portuguese social and cultural life to be controlled by a single, definitive, and clear-cut group considering itself biologically pure (*sangre limpia*) or culturally perfect according to either European or African standards. There were dramatic conflicts between those who had Christianity and Latin as their ideal of perfection and those who were fanatical followers of Mohammed or Moses. But the general result of the long contact of the Spanish and Portuguese peoples with the Arabs, the Moors, and the Jews was one of integration, or balance, of contending elements rather than of segregation, or sharp differentiation, of any of them or violent conflict between them.

The Arabs added to the Spanish and Portuguese languages a rich vocabulary of Arabisms, through which some sociological conclusions may be reached. One of these is that in both languages Arabisms seem to outnumber Latinisms among old scientific and technical terms of importance, related to agriculture and land industries. And some popular expressions, as "to work hard like a Moor," seem to explain why certain parts of the peninsula are considered "fertile soil" by Arabian authors and "arid land" by Christian ones. A significant detail is that in the Portuguese language the word for olive tree, *oliveira*, is of Latin origin whereas the current word for the commercial product of the same tree—*azeite*, oil—is of Arab origin. Other examples might be added to suggest how Arabs and Latins, Christians and Jews, Catholics and Mohammedans have formed the Spanish and Portuguese culture (for it is really *one* culture composed of various subcultures), the Spanish and Portuguese languages, and the Spanish and Portuguese ethnic types—more or less harmonious, more or less contradictory products of a sort of competitive co-operation between different human (and perhaps ethnic) capacities and culturally diverse specialized talents and antagonistic dispositions.

Regional diversity in peninsular conditions of soil, of geographical situation, and of climate should also be taken into consideration by the student of the European background of Brazilian history, a background that is not purely European but also African; not purely Christian but also Jewish and Mohammedan; not only agrarian (as illustrated by the importance of the farmers in the earlier days of Portugal) but also military; not only industrial (as developed by the Arabs and the Moors) but maritime and commercial (as developed by

Nordics and Jews); marked not only by the capacity for hard, continuous, and monotonous work and by the inclination towards sedentary farm life, but also by the spirit of adventure and romantic chivalry. The diversity of physical conditions is only less important in Spanish and Portuguese history than is the dramatic diversity of ethnic and cultural elements as a key to understanding why such tremendous forces for absolute uniformity of culture, character, and life as a violent centralization of political power in Lisbon (or in Madrid), the Inquisition or the Society of Jesus, and as, after the discovery of Brazil, such a brutal and efficient one-man dictatorship as that of the Marquis of Pombal in Portugal, were not able to destroy differences, variety, spontaneous popular vigour among the Portuguese.

These forces for uniformity were probably essential to the development not only of Spain but of Portugal as efficient colonizing powers; but it is certainly a good sign of social vitality in each that neither of them became strictly orthodox or Catholic in the religious and social sense desired by the Jesuits or the Inquisition; that neither of them lost its regional and cultural diversity under the pressure of strongly centralized government. For the preservation of such healthy differences or antagonisms, it was a good thing that the forces for uniformity did not always act together but were sometimes competitive or antagonistic: the Crown against the Church, for instance; the Society of Jesus against the Inquisition. There was a period when the Jews themselves had the Jesuits as their protectors against the powerful Inquisition. And the fact is that, though nominally expelled, the Jews did not disappear from Portuguese life.

As a very competent student of Portuguese cultural history, Mr. Aubrey F. G. Bell, reminds us, Sobieski, a Polish traveller, wrote in 1611: "There are in Portugal very many Jews, so many that various houses in Portugal have a Jewish origin. Although they have burnt and expelled them, many live hidden among the Portuguese." [3] When it became fashionable in Portugal during the seventeenth and the eighteenth centuries for gentlemen to wear glasses in order to look wise and learned, shrewd Sephardic Jews were able to disguise their Semitic noses under spectacles. And Christians and Jews alike seem to have used rings set with precious stones to show their disdain for manual labour—a custom that survived in Brazil. The display of nobility by Portuguese aristocrats, both Christian and Jew—for the Jews in Portugal and Spain were an aristocracy rather than a plutocracy—sometimes assumed grotesque forms, as when three gentlemen formed a partnership in the use of the same silk suit, two of them having to stay at home when the third went out. A traveller tells us of Jewish physicians, disguised as Christians, in Portuguese America in the seventeenth century who prescribed pork so as to lessen the suspicion of the charge of Judaism. And they all were noted for their attention to

3. *Portugal of the Portuguese* (London, 1915), p. 4.

dress, even when working as carriers or engaging in other humble occupations, like the Sephardic sellers of *"pan de España"* in Smyrna.

Sometimes the King of Portugal himself was the one who protected the Jews of his kingdom against a too strict enforcement of laws against them, laws based on an ideal of religious rather than of racial purity. Such an ideal would have considerable political importance in the foundation and development of Brazil as a politically orthodox colony of Portugal. There was a time in Brazil when friars came to meet new comers in their boats, not to ascertain their nationality or inspect police papers or examine their physical health, but to inquire into their religious health: Were they Christian? Were their parents Christian? How orthodox were they? As immigration authorities at the service of the State as well as the Church, the friars were guarding against the danger, not of contagious disease or of a criminal disposition, but of infidelity or heresy. The heretic was considered a political enemy of Portuguese America: if he was a Jew he had to disguise himself as a New Christian and remain a Jew secretly; if a Protestant, he had to disguise himself as a Catholic. It seems, however, that there was considerable accommodation in the adjustment of such differences as far as the rich Jews were concerned.

The Jews were an important element in Portugal's social and cultural life, not only for their commercial activity and their capacity to establish cosmopolitan contacts for the Lusitanian Christian adventurers when their maritime enterprises began, but for other things as well. One should not forget that for such enterprises the Portuguese were particularly favoured by their geographical situation; or that from their remote beginning they were greatly influenced by the sea. Some authors refer to that portion of the Atlantic Ocean which lies between the west coast of Portugal and a line drawn through the Azores to Madeira as "the Lusitanian Sea"; and Dalgado, a specialist in climatic geography, reminds us of the fact that, taken as a whole, the "Lusitanian Sea" has more currents than any other sea in Europe—a fact that explains, he adds, "the quantity and the variety of fishes to be found in it."[4] Another specialist in the subject, Kohl, more than half a century ago styled Portugal the "Netherlands of the Iberian Peninsula," a comparison likewise made by Fischer, the author of a map showing the configuration of the Hispanic peninsula. Dalgado describes Portugal as "the Western Inclined Plane of the Iberian peninsula, for it is the exposure of the large portion of its surface to the oceanic winds on the western side that gives it its distinctive climate."[5] Not only, one might add, its distinctive climate from the point of view of physical geography, but also its distinctive historical and cultural climate. For the ethnic and cultural history of Portugal, the heterogeneous ethnic composition of its population, and its commercial and urban cosmopolitanism in opposition to its agrarian or rural conservatism are all

4. D. G. Dalgado, *The Climate of Portugal* (Lisbon, 1914), p. 33.
5. *Ibid.*, p. 42.

The European Background

connected with Portugal's being the "Western Inclined Plane of the Iberian Peninsula."

Certain anthropologists consider the Iberians to have been the original inhabitants of the Hispanic peninsula, and some describe them as mongoloid. But so many intruders have settled in Portugal—the Ligurians, the Celts and the Gauls, the Phoenicians, the Carthaginians, the Romans, the Suevi and the Goths, the Jews, the Moors, the Germans, the French, the English—that it would be difficult to find a modern people whose recent and remote ethnic and cultural past is more heterogeneous. It should be added that, before Brazil was discovered and its colonization begun, the population of Portugal had been coloured by the introduction of a considerable number of Negroes,[6] used as domestic slaves, and of some East Indians, noted for their talent as wood-carvers and cabinet-makers.

With such a heterogeneous ethnic and cultural past, the diversity shown by the Portuguese both as anthropological and as cultural types is not surprising. Some students of the Portuguese ethos regard the Phoenicians, the Carthaginians, and the Jews as the source of the spirit of maritime enterprise that flourished in Portugal from the fourteenth to the seventeenth centuries. They also point out that the Romans gave the Portuguese the bony structure of their language and of some of their social institutions; and that the Moors left many a trait

---

6. L. S. Silva Rebello, *Memoria sobre a população e a agricultura de Portugal desde a fundação da monarchia até 1865* (Lisbon, 1865), p. 60.

of influence, not only in social institutions and in the language, music, and dances of Portugal, but also in its material culture—architecture, industrial technique, cuisine, and popular dress. The presence and influence in Portugal of French and English Crusaders with their spirit of adventure and their disdain for agricultural labour; the presence and influence there of the Jews, with their commercial spirit and (since they were Sephardic Jews) their disdain for all kinds of manual labour and their excessive enthusiasm for the intellectual and bureaucratic professions; the Portuguese victories over the Moors; the conquests of the Portuguese in Asia and in Africa and the opportunity to employ Negroes, East Indians, and Moors to work in the fields and in the manual arts—all these factors seem to have developed in a large part of the Portuguese population the spirit of adventure and the aristocratic prejudices that appeared among some of the first men to come from Portugal to America. In Portuguese America these prejudices took the form of love of military action, of show and grandeur, and of bureaucratic occupation or parasitism, along with slave-making activities, first directed again the Indians and later concentrated in the importation of Africans to work on the almost feudal plantations that some Portuguese were able to establish in Brazil. Fortunately for both Portugal and Brazil such acquired tastes did not destroy entirely in the Portuguese of the old, rural stock—in the so-called *portugueses velhos*, who would be the basic human element

The European Background 13

of the agrarian colonization of Brazil—their traditional love of agriculture. Men like Duarte Coelho and the Albuquerques brought from Portugal to Brazil, in addition to the spirit of adventure, a feeling for social continuity and a capacity for long, patient, and difficult labour. They loved trees and rural life. They were, by tradition, gentlemen farmers or planters. Duarte descended from the agricultural nobility of the North of Portugal, as did his wife, Dona Brites, who became the first woman governor in America. From the same region there migrated to Brazil a number of families who followed Duarte and Dona Brites, some related to them. The Portuguese peasants of that region—the North Atlantic region—are generally considered rather dull of intellect, though religious, musical, occasionally gay, patient, and hard-working.

But the Portuguese of the old rural stock who came to Brazil in the sixteenth century would have been incomplete or one-sided without the so-called "enemies of agriculture," whose predominating traits were their spirit of adventure, their love of novelties, their cleverness, their commercial and urban spirit, their genius for trade. The farmers with a deep love for the land and a thorough knowledge of agriculture were sometimes abused or exploited in Brazil by those of their fellow countrymen whose passion was for commercial adventure and for urban life—most of them probably Jews; but this antagonism was, in more than one respect, beneficial to Portuguese America. Urban Jews with a genius for trade made possible the industrialization of sugarcane agriculture in Brazil and the successful commercialization of Brazilian sugar.

This antagonism, however, must be regarded by the student of early Brazilian history not only as an evil—for it was an evil—but as a stimulus to differentiation and progress. One of the most capable interpreters of Portuguese economic history, Senhor Antonio Sergio, has made sufficiently clear that the commercial class in Portugal, the business men of the coast line, became more important than the aristocratic proprietors of the hinterland in shaping, with the King's co-operation, a national, or rather an international, policy that neglected the hinterland to foster maritime adventure. The process has been carefully studied by J. Lucio de Azevedo, the best authority on the economic history of Portugal.[7] I hardly do more than summarize what Sergio suggests and Azevedo explains when I say that the early rise of the commercial classes in Portugal is a fact never to be overlooked by the student of the European background of Brazilian history. As Sergio reminds us, Lisbon became the seaport where the commerce of the North of Europe met that of the South; it was due to this tendency towards maritime commerce and the concentration of attention on the seaports that the problem of peopling the southern part of Portugal, where agriculture has always depended on expensive irrigation, began to be neglected at an early stage. Since the chief aim of European commerce at this time was, as every-

7. *Epocas de Portugal Economico* (Lisbon, 1929).

The European Background 15

one knows, the acquisition of oriental products, the Portuguese business men of Lisbon, some of them Jews or connected with Jews, took advantage of the geographical situation of their town and also of the fact that feudalism was not so powerful in Portugal as in other parts of Europe to become masters of the national policy and to transform it into a bold cosmopolitan, commercial, and at the same time imperial adventure, through scientific and quasi-scientific efforts to discover new routes for commerce, new lands and new markets to be exploited, and pagan populations not only to be converted into Christians but also to be subdued into Portuguese subjects or slaves. The King of Portugal himself became "the Merchant of Merchants" and the state officials also turned traders.[8]

It is well known that in the fourteenth and fifteenth centuries, with the irruption of the Turks into the eastern seaports of the Mediterranean and because of other difficulties, the need for a sea-route to India became acutely felt in Europe. No European nation was in a more advantageous position to solve this grave problem than semi-European Portugal, a nation so precociously maritime and commercial in its political program that, as early as the latter part of the fourteenth century, laws were enacted by King Dom Fernando which gave special protection to maritime commerce and encouraged naval construction; which gave more

---

8. Antonio Sergio, *A Sketch of the History of Portugal*, trans. from the Portuguese by Constantino José dos Santos (Lisbon, 1928), p. 88.

assistance to such a cause than to the noble proprietors of latifundia, especially of lands regained from the Moors—lands that needed irrigation, then considered a matter of royal aid or something about the economic capacity of the not too wealthy proprietors. It seems that such aid was never given. In not assisting the aristocratic proprietors of latifundia, the kings of Portugal perhaps had in view the definite and efficient development of centralized royal power, which might be endangered by a strong land aristocracy.

The policy of disdain or neglect of the Portuguese hinterland followed by some of the most influential kings of Portugal like Dom Fernando explains why so many noblemen began to come to Lisbon as candidates for government appointments. And, as such, even they grew enthusiastic over maritime adventure, trade, naval construction; they became co-operators, rather than enemies, of the merchant princes of the seaports when the sea-route to India was opened and parts of the East became colonies or semi-colonies of Portugal. Some of these aristocrats went to Brazil, appointed by the Portuguese Crown to high bureaucratic positions or military posts, or sent on special missions that required from them the best of their military experience and of their capacity as leaders. There they encountered such mutually antagonistic but also co-operative forces as the King, the Church, the Jews, the common man, the heretic, and the political or common criminals forced to leave Portugal and go to Brazil.

It seems to me that some authors—Sombart is one of

The European Background 17

them—over-emphasize the importance of the Jews in Portuguese maritime and colonial enterprises, including the development of Brazil as a sugar-producing colony. Nevertheless one should not go to the opposite extreme: that of overlooking the part played by the Jews in the cultural development of Portugal and in the definitely cosmopolitan shape taken by its economic policy after the days of Dom Fernando. For Portuguese kings and Jewish princes of finance understood each other so well that Jews had been royal tax-collectors since the early days of the Portuguese monarchy; and under some of the best kings Sephardic Jews were ministers of finance, royal physicians, royal astrologers. Under Portuguese royal protection Jewish merchants are said to have become proud and conceited; to have adorned their horses with tassels; to have indulged in luxury. And one can imagine what powerful rivals of the Catholic chaplains, confessors, advisers, and educators they became as royal physicians, astrologers, and tax-collectors. For in those days a man's body was becoming again almost as important as his soul, and shrewd astrologers seemed to be able to guide a king or a queen, a prince or a captain, through mysterious regions of this world and of the next—regions entirely unknown to Catholic masters of theology and divinity.

For those who study the history of Portugal from a Brazilian point of view it is interesting to follow Jewish activities in connection with the maritime and commercial enterprises that had sugar-producing in Brazil as their by-product, if not their chief product. From the reign of King Sancho II, who was interested in the development of the Portuguese navy, the Jews were obliged to pay a navy tax: for each ship fitted out by the King they had to provide "an anchor and a new anchor-tow sixty ells long or instead to make a money payment of 60 livres." They controlled, among other branches of commerce, the food supply, and more than once we are reminded by such students of the history of Jewish activities in Portugal as Azevedo that they were accused, with or without reason, of holding up supplies in order to raise prices—a practice not peculiar to Portuguese Jews of the fourteenth and fifteenth centuries.

According to some authors, at the root of the ability of the Portuguese to acclimatize themselves in various parts of the world better than almost any other Europeans, lies the great admixture of the people of Portugal with the Semitic race; and not the Jews alone but the Moors also would have contributed to that special capacity. Against such a generalization there stands a fact of considerable importance: that "New Lusitania"—the north-eastern part of Brazil—was settled mostly by men and women from northern Portugal, a population noted for its Romano-Visigothic blood and "Nordic" characteristics. Such men and women, some of them from the agricultural nobility, could adapt themselves well to the tropical climate of that Brazilian region where sugar-cane was made the basis for a revival of feudal social organization, with Africans as slaves. Perhaps the Portuguese climate itself—a climate more African than

The European Background 19

European—best explains why the Portuguese adapt themselves better than other Europeans to tropical climates. And one should not forget that, during the first generations of settlers of the tropical parts of Brazil, this adaptation was based on slave work; the Portuguese did not themselves do the hardest work in the fields but had Indians and later Negroes as plantation slaves.

It is to be noted that it was not Brazil that made the Portuguese masters in the art of living and sometimes of fortunes based on slavery: when the colonization of Brazil began, Portugal itself was full of African slaves —though this, of course, was only a miniature of what was to develop in Brazil on a large, almost monumental, scale. But when they reached Brazil, most of the Portuguese already had a love of display and grandeur and a distaste for manual work that are to be explained, in large part, by their having had, for nearly a century, most of their domestic work done by Negro slaves and, for many centuries, some of the most difficult agricultural labour provided by the Moors.

To the Portuguese the Moors had been not only the efficient agricultural workers who knew how to transform arid lands into gardens, as if by a miracle, but a dark race who had not always been the serfs but sometimes were the masters of a large part of the Iberian peninsula. Portuguese of the purest Nordic blood had found in brown Moorish women, some of them princesses, the supreme revelation of feminine beauty. As more than one student of Brazilian history has pointed out—in particular the American Mr. Roy Nash, whose book *The Conquest of Brazil* is one of the best ever written on Brazil from a sociological standpoint—the first contact of the Portuguese or the Spanish with a darker-skinned people had been "the contact of the conquered with their brown-skinned conquerors." And "the darker man was the more cultured, more learned, more artistic. He lived in castles and occupied the towns. He was the rich man and the Portuguese became serfs upon his land. Under such conditions, it would be deemed an honor for the white to marry or mate with the governing class, the brown man, instead of the reverse." [9]

Through the sociological study of the famous Portuguese legend of the *moura encantada*, I reached years ago the same conclusion as Mr. Roy Nash: that the idealization, by the Portuguese people, of the brown woman, or the Moorish girl or woman, as the supreme type of human beauty had probably a very important effect on the direction taken by their relations with Indian (Amerindian) women in Brazil. Mystic, poetical, given to dreams about their past, lovers of beautiful plants as well as of useful and commercial ones, the Portuguese have peopled some of their woods and fountains with fascinating legends of Moorish princesses. The boy who is fortunate enough to discover and treat well the animal or the plant which is only a disguise for some beautiful Moorish princess of the past will marry her and be rich and happy. And in all such stories and legends the Moorish brown girl is regarded as the su-

9. *The Conquest of Brazil* (New York, 1926), p. 37.

preme type of beauty and of sexual attractiveness; the Moors are considered superior, and not inferior, to the purely white Portuguese.

Such legends are still active among the Portuguese peasants, a large majority of whom are illiterate. Portuguese children of all classes grow up under the spell of such non-European or non-"Aryan" legends and myths. One can imagine how active the pro-Moorish legends were among the Portuguese who in the sixteenth century first came into contact with the Indians in America, another brown race. Their historical experience, their folk-lore, their popular literature in prose and verse—all these voices from their past told the Portuguese who first arrived in Brazil that brown people are not always inferior to white people.

Legends are a living force among illiterate peasants like those of Portugal; and legends may express a truth more effective and enduring than some of the ever-changing half-truths taught by pedants rather than by scholars. Illiteracy among peasants with a rich folk-lore or folk heritage like that of Spain and Portugal does not necessarily mean ignorance but may be intimately connected with wisdom, imagination, and humour. From their legends most of the Portuguese who discovered and colonized Brazil knew that a brown people may be superior to a white people, as the Moors had been in Portugal and Spain; and from their long contact with the Moors, considered in that part of Europe not an inferior but a superior race, the Portuguese assimilated many mores and conceptions: the Moorish ideal of feminine beauty (a fat woman), the Moorish taste for concubinage or polygamy, the tolerance and consideration of both races for mixed-bloods, their conception of domestic slaves as almost a sort of poor relation kept at home. The Portuguese in Brazil retained many marks of Moorish influence in their not too strictly European nor too strictly Christian moral and social behaviour. This was especially true of the common men, though in general it applies to Portuguese of all classes.

I wish to say more about the illiterate peasants of Portugal, to whom Brazil owes so much. Since the early days of the sixteenth century they have been the continuous basic element for the development of a real new culture—not a merely sub-European or colonial one—in that part of the American continent. As James Murphy [10] and more recent foreign observers in Portugal have found out, the illiterate peasants are the flower or the cream of that nation; and from more than one point of view they—and not the noblemen, the bourgeois, the finely educated—have been the flower and the cream of the Portuguese colonization of Brazil.

A number of Brazilian anecdotes and jokes are directed at the Portuguese peasants: about how naïve or rustic they are; how ignorant of technical progress; how stupid or dull some of them are by contrast with other Europeans or with the native or mestizo Brazilian —the *carioca*, the *caboclo*, the *amarelinho* (who is, of course, the supreme hero of many Brazilian stories). In these anecdotes the Portuguese peasant is not neces-

10. *Travels in Portugal* (London, 1795).

The European Background 23

sarily the villain—indeed he never is really the villain. But, being generally represented as stout, naïve, and childlike, and also as sexually potent as primitive men are supposed to be in contrast with the too civilized ones, he is made by Brazilian legend a sort of ridiculous but lovable Falstaff. The caricature merely emphasizes his ignorance in the face of an urban and technical progress which naturally is entirely strange to men from a predominantly pastoral and agricultural country like Portugal.

Since the sixteenth century, Portuguese peasants have brought with them to Brazil a wealth of legends, of incantations, of folk-songs, of popular literature in verse and prose, of popular arts; and it is mainly through them —illiterate peasants and artisans—rather than through the erudite or the learned, that similar popular or folk values from the Indians and the Negroes have been assimilated by Portuguese America and become the source for a new culture: the Brazilian culture.

Some students of modern cultures tend to exaggerate the importance of literacy. Reading and writing are means of communication very useful for industrial civilizations and for merely political forms of democratic organization—though, at that, they are apparently being superseded by the telephone, the radio, and television. Such countries as China, India, Mexico, and Brazil will probably not have the same need for literacy as a means of achieving modernization as had the vast masses during the nineteenth century and even Soviet Russia at the beginning of this century.

Mr. Aubrey F. G. Bell, who knows Portugal familiarly, writes that "thrice fortunate" are they who "can associate and converse with the Portuguese peasants during the summer *romaria* or village *festa*, or as they sit round the winter fire (*a lareira*), or gather for some great common task, a shearing (*tosquia*) or *esfolhada* (separating the maize cob from its sheath), for they are certain to glean a rich store of proverbs, folklore, and philology," and goes on to state that "it may be said without exaggeration that the Portuguese people, for all its colossal ignorance and lack of letters, is one of the most civilized and intelligent in Europe."[11] In saying this he is paying the greatest tribute that the son of a highly industrial and mechanical civilization such as the British can pay to a people often ridiculed for its backwardness. That this backwardness is no evidence of low intelligence or inferior race is the opinion of the most careful students of the Portuguese people and of Portuguese history.

Noblemen, kings, merchant princes, doctors of philosophy, law, and medicine, priests, Sephardic Jews, scholars, and scientists have contributed brilliantly to the Portuguese colonization of Brazil. But it should be repeated that the most constant creative force in it has probably been the illiterate peasants, some of them men with North African blood: Arabian, Moorish, and even Negro. It is the result of their work that may be presented today to the world as one of the most successful

11. *Op. cit.*, p. 15.

The European Background 25

colonizing efforts, not so much of Europeans, but of semi-Europeans, in tropical America.

The Portuguese common man was present in the first Portuguese colonizing efforts in Brazil; a recent careful study of documents of that period has shown that a number of Portuguese founders of *paulista* families in southern Brazil—families later famous for their pioneer work in central, northern, and the extreme parts of southern Brazil—were artisans or peasants. Portuguese artisans seem to have come in a considerable number in the sixteenth century to Bahia, the first town of importance built in Brazil; some of them were paid very high wages. They soon became numerous in Pernambuco as small-town merchants and artisans, rivals of the second and third generation of descendants of the noblemen and gentlemen farmers from the North of Portugal who, with the help or assistance of rich Jews, had founded the sugar industry in Brazil. Later, in 1620, two hundred Portuguese families arrived in Maranhão from the Azores. In 1626 others came to Pará, and in the eighteenth century a large number established themselves in Rio Grande do Sul. They were not noblemen but peasants and artisans, common men whose mediocre success in agricultural colonization is explained by the fact that the feudal system prevailing in large areas of Portuguese America made it almost impossible for common men to prosper as farmers. If Portuguese agricultural colonists established in Pará (Nossa Senhora do Ó and other places), in Bahia (Sinimbú, Engenho Novo,

Rio Pardo), and in Rio de Janeiro did not succeed remarkably as agriculturists, it must be pointed out that even less successful were the Irish peasants established also as farmers in the interior of Bahia and the German families located early in the nineteenth century in the interior of Pernambuco; indeed, these were magnificent failures. But as soon as they were able to escape from a feudal system of land domination in which there was hardly any place for a genuine farmer or an independent agriculturist, most of those Portuguese agriculturists found jobs as artisans or prospered as traders in coast cities, where so many of them have been strikingly successful as merchants and founders of new industries.

In his very interesting *New Viewpoints on the Spanish Colonization of America* Professor Silvio Zavala tells us that Philip II permitted Portuguese farmers to emigrate to Spanish America [12]—perhaps, I venture to suggest, because the conditions were more favourable to farmers in some areas of Spanish America than in most areas of Portuguese America. According to Professor Zavala, colonization of a military character had spread over Spanish America; but a large part of Portuguese America was dominated from the sixteenth to the nineteenth century by a feudal type of colonization even more alien to the ordinary European farmer than was the purely military one. And in both Hispanic Americas, the Portuguese and the Spanish, there developed another type of privileged colonization whose interests

---

12. *New Viewpoints on the Spanish Colonization of America* (Philadelphia, 1943), p. 110.

did not coincide with those of the ordinary colonists —that of the Jesuits, whose policy it was to segregate the Indians and even to compete agriculturally and commercially with the ordinary colonists through using Indian (Amerindian) labour that most of the civilian community did not obtain so easily or freely as the Jesuits, though it was taxed to support them. Privileged as they were under most of the kings of Portugal and Spain during the most decisive phase of colonization of America, the Jesuits did extraordinarily valuable work in Brazil as missionaries and educators; but their excessively paternalistic and even autocratic system of educating the Indians ran counter to the early tendencies of Brazil's development as an ethnic democracy. This point—so clearly seen, from the Spanish-American democratic point of view, by Las Casas, when he wished to utilize colonization by farmers "who should live by tilling the rich lands of the Indies, lands which the Indian owners would voluntarily grant to them," lands where "the Spaniards would intermarry with the natives and make of both peoples one of the best commonwealths in the world and perhaps one of the most Christian and peaceful" [13]—was also clearly seen, from a Brazilian point of view, by José Bonifacio, leader of the movement for the independence of Portuguese America. He realized the danger of a native policy of isolation like the one followed for some time by the Jesuits in Brazil—danger to the development of Brazil as a democratic community—and he therefore advocated

13. *Ibid.*, pp. 110–111.

the practice of racial crossing and cultural interpenetration until, under the inspiration of his ideas, a comprehensive plan for dealing with the Indians was adopted by the Emperor of Brazil in 1845. Following a tradition that has its roots in ideas held by the Portuguese kings and statesmen, sometimes in opposition to the Jesuits, the plan included the promotion of intermarriage between the Portuguese and the Indian, of instruction, and of assistance in the form of housing, tools, clothing, and medicine. It also included the right of natives to acquire title to land outside reservations.

If privileged types of colonization have prevented the majority of Portuguese common men who have emigrated to America from becoming conquerors there and owners of virgin areas of good agricultural lands, they seem to have found compensation for this repression of their "possessive" rather than "creative" instincts in their really extraordinary procreative activity as polygamous males. Some of them became famous, like João Ramalho in the sixteenth century, for their many children from Indian women. As such they became the rivals, the equals, sometimes the triumphant competitors of Portuguese *fidalgos,* or noblemen, like Jeronymo de Albuquerque, whose addiction to polygamy marks them as inheriting Moorish rather than European and Christian traditions of sexual morality. Such excesses, profitable to Brazil from the point of view of a purely quantitative colonization, were not always beneficial to the development of a Christian family life in Portuguese America. Against them not only the Jesuits, but Church

The European Background 29

authorities as well, more than once made their voices heard.

Every student of the social history of Brazil knows that, for an adequate knowledge of this subject (as for that of the social origins and social development of other modern nations), the gathering of sufficient information on the life, the activity, and the influence of the masses of the people is a task still remaining to be done. Information on the basic social and cultural contacts between human groups producing modern civilization is still incomplete. As has been remarked by an American student of social history, Professor Dwight Sanderson, the available sources have often emphasized political structures and documentary evidence, while students of mythology and folk-lore not infrequently go to the other extreme in their evaluation of cultural survivals and of the common people's contributions to the development of modern culture or civilization. Hence the need of a re-study of some problems of European and American history from a sociological standpoint.

Portugal and the Portuguese colonization of Brazil need such a re-study, based on a new evaluating of the Portuguese contribution to modern civilization. This contribution was perhaps made in larger part by the merchant, the missionary, the common man, the intellectual, the scientist, and the woman who followed her husband in his overseas adventures, than by the *conquistador*, the military leader, the statesman, the bishops, or the kings—even though Portugal, in its most creative phase (that is, during the fifteenth and the sixteenth centuries), was remarkable for its far-seeing, energetic, and capable kings, princes, and statesmen.

During the fifteenth and sixteenth centuries the Portuguese—most of them engaged in trade—enriched European civilization with a number of plants and cultural values and techniques assimilated from Asia and Africa. Portuguese America was also benefited by these, for it was Portuguese merchants who introduced into Europe (or were among the first Europeans to introduce or reintroduce) a taste for the following things: sugar, tea, rice pudding, pepper, and cinnamon; the guinea fowl; the parasol, the umbrella, and the palanquin; porcelain and Arabian tiles; the veranda (of the East Indies); concave roofs, rounded cornices, and pagoda-like summer houses; Chinese gardens and fans; oriental rugs and perfumes. And as early as the sixteenth century the same merchants took to Brazil some of these tastes and luxuries, as well as silks and jewels. They were the pioneers of modern international trade between the orient and the occident, between the Old World and the New.

North Europeans, who have made of the daily bath a supreme technique in modern domestic comfort, scorn the Portuguese peasant for not taking so many baths as they do; but it was Portuguese navigators and traders who were among the first Europeans to bring from the East the almost un-Christian (and certainly un-European) habit of the daily bath—which in Europe was at first, and to some extent is still, a luxury reserved to ladies and gentlemen. Though the Portuguese are ridiculed today for using toothpicks at the dinner table,

The European Background 31

it was probably a Portuguese who brought from China to Europe the first porcelain for the tea of the sophisticated. The Portuguese were, also, probably the first Europeans to bring, from the East to Europe, East Indian cotton textiles, especially calicoes, thus revolutionizing social habits and cultural behaviour in the European Christian countries. For, as every student of modern European civilization knows, the cheap East Indian cottons increased the use of underclothes, thereby "improving both health and cleanliness." [14] And the Portuguese started yet another social and cultural revolution, this one in the orient, when they introduced into Japan the European Jesuits (including the great Francis Xavier), European muskets, and possibly syphilis.

The Portuguese also made their new colony known in Europe for its beautiful plants like the evening primrose, its useful woods like Brazil-wood and rosewood, its delicious fruits like the pineapple, its fine Bahia tobacco, its Pará or Brazil nuts, its Amazonian rubber, its hammocks made by the Indians, and its plants with medicinal properties like ipecacuanha. Soon after the discovery of Brazil, the Portuguese began to study Bra-

14. Shepard Bancroft Clough and Charles Woolsey Cole, *Economic History of Europe* (Boston, 1941), p. 263. See also Adolphe Reischwein, *China and Europe* (London, 1915), pp. 61–67. James Edward Gillespie, *The Influence of Overseas Expansion on England (1500-1700)* (New York, 1920); Ramalho Ortigão, *O Culto da Arte em Portugal* (Lisbon, 1896); Edgar Prestage, *The Portuguese Pioneers* (London, 1934); and Gilberto Freyre, *O Mundo que o Portugues Creou* (Rio, 1940) also discuss the subject and point out aspects of the Portuguese influence in the social and cultural life of Europe as a result of Portuguese contacts with Africa, the orient, and America.

zilian plants and animals, and especially Indian or Amerindian customs and foods with an accuracy that has been praised by modern scientists. They also began to build in tropical America houses of a new type and with extra-European characteristics, houses whose architecture exhibited a combination of Asiatic and African modes with traditional European styles. They began to develop a Luso-Brazilian cookery based on their European traditions adapted to American conditions and resources, and also on their experience with the plants and the culinary processes of Asia and Africa.

The Portuguese are also associated not only with the introduction into or popularization in Europe of Brazilian sugar, under the name of *mascavado* or *muscovado*, but also with the dissemination of the use of tobacco as an aristocratic custom among Europeans. As a result of the use of tobacco—from Brazil and other parts of America—it seems that the Europeans in general, and the Portuguese in particular, began to spit more than before; and it is significant that the English word *cuspidor* comes from the Portuguese verb *cuspir*, to spit. But this is not the only word that has come from the Portuguese, or, through the Portuguese, from East Indian, African, Asiatic, and American languages into the English and other European languages. Numerous words of Portuguese origin indicate how important a part Portugal played in the pioneer days of modern international trade: *bamboo* (the tree), *veranda* (for porch), *caravel* (a type of vessel), *tapioca* (the starch

The European Background 33

of "mandioca"), *pagoda* (a tower-like structure), *kraal* (a type of African village), *muscovado* (a type of sugar), *cobra* (snake), *cobra-de-capelo* (an East Indian snake), *jararaca* (a serpent), *jacaranda* (Brazilian rosewood), *caste* (a hereditary and endogamous social group), *palanquin* (the Asiatic sedan chair largely used in Brazil), *cashew* or *cajou* (a nut), *jaguar* (a large feline of Latin America), *samba* (an Afro-Brazilian dance), *mango* (an East Indian fruit now very common in Brazil), *Port* and *Madeira* (types of wine), *canja* (a thick soup of chicken and rice, highly praised by Theodore Roosevelt),[15] *cruzado* (a Portuguese coin mentioned by Shakespeare), and *valorization*, a "Portuguesism" in the English language denoting a technique for the commercial protection of a product, a technique used first by Brazilians in connection with their coffee and since then by other peoples in connection with various other commodities. And it is my belief that *pickanniny* comes not from the Spanish, as generally stated by dictionaries and by Mr. H. L. Mencken in *The American Language*, but from the Portuguese word *pequenino*. *Formosa* (the name of the important island off the coast of China) is also a Portuguese word, not Spanish. These words are a few evidences of Portuguese ubiquity prior to the colonization of Brazil or contemporaneous with it.

15. *Through the Brazilian Wilderness* (New York, 1914), p. 165. Theodore Roosevelt introduced also into the English language a number of Portuguese-Amerindian names of animals like *tamanduá-bandeira* and *piranha*.

In dealing with the European background of Brazilian history from a sociological standpoint, one is led to the somewhat paradoxical conclusion that it was not an entirely European background: it was also Asiatic and African.

II

FRONTIER AND PLANTATION IN BRAZIL

From its very beginning, the history of Brazil was marked by two apparently contradictory tendencies that, in fact, were complementary to each other. I refer to the mobility of those groups of men who expanded Portuguese America towards the North, South, and West in contrast to the permanent settling, with satisfaction or delight, near the Atlantic sea coast, from Maranhão to São Vicente, by other social and perhaps biological types of men: those who came from Portugal with enough capital to establish themselves as slave-holding sugar-cane planters and to live on their plantations almost like feudal lords.

These sugar-cane planters, even more than the men who dug the soil for gold, were the *vertical* founders of Brazil in the sense that some of them rooted themselves deeply in the land and built for themselves and for their families and sometimes for their slaves, not cabins or huts, but solid stone or brick houses. These mansions soon took the name of "big houses." The slave quarters were given an African name: *senzalas*. The planters also built their churches or chapels and their sugar-mills of the same noble and enduring material as their mansions, and sometimes surrounded them with noble and long-lived trees imported from Asia, Africa, and Europe: palm trees, mango trees, jaca trees; by noble and useful animals also imported from older civilizations: horses, cows, cats.

The *horizontal* founders were the continuously migratory men. Though heterogeneous, these were mostly men whose spirit of adventure and love of individual freedom were too strong to let them settle down on the coast and live comfortably in the neighbourhood of churches and official buildings where taxes soon began to be collected by representatives of the Portuguese Crown. Nor did they like to live in the shadow of schools maintained by puritanical priests and of ecclesiastical courts presided over by representatives of the Holy Inquisition—courts anxious to detect and punish religious heresy and sexual irregularity among the colonists.

By pushing on to the extreme South or the extreme North, by going to the West in search of gold and of Indians to sell to the planters as slaves, the migratory men escaped the influence of the feudal social organization established on the coast by the sedentary men. These latter had brought from Portugal a social status that was not only maintained in Brazil but improved by them with the rapid prosperity of the cane agriculture and the sugar industry in that part of America.

While the majority of the migratory men, or frontiers-men, were simple and even rustic in their social tastes and habits and had no stable form of domestic

Frontier and Plantation 37

architecture—only huts almost as primitive as those of the Indians, whose diet and methods of nomadic agriculture they also copied—some of the sugar-cane planters developed or maintained in Brazil lordly manners, able as they were to support aristocratic establishments and to enjoy a diet almost entirely European; indeed, a number of them persisted for years in importing from Portugal their wines and much of their food, as well as fashionable dress for both sexes.

While the migratory men, like all bold pioneers, enjoyed in the wilderness a freedom of action that included a remarkable and most un-Christian liberty to have many women, the plantation master was at no disadvantage with the frontiers-man in this respect, since without leaving his own lands he could have as many women as he wished, besides the legitimate one he had brought from Portugal or to whom he had been properly married in Brazil. It is true that orthodox priests, especially the Jesuits, denounced such abuses or irregularities and preached against them. But it should not be forgotten that one of the characteristics of the feudal, aristocratic plantation system that developed in Brazil was the almost absolute power of the sugar-planters. Privileged as they were by the King, they were able to become real feudal lords and, as such, to defend the cause and the interests of Portugal against savages and against rival European powers. Every time that a planter acted *pro domo sua* he was acting also in favour of Portuguese power in America. For the white mansions, or "big houses," became, even more than the public buildings, symbols of Portuguese stability in the coastal areas of Brazil. They became also the physical expression of a new type of feudal or patriarchal power that through isolation and self-sufficiency was to develop into a strong spirit of independence and even rebellion against the Crown and republicanism.

The Crown privileges explain why the "big houses" became not only more important than most of the public buildings, but also more important than the cathedrals, the individual churches, and the purely religious monasteries. I say "individual churches" because each big house or mansion had its own church or chapel as part of its architectural and social complex, with a chaplain who was dependent upon the plantation master, or senhor—more dependent upon him than upon his bishop; and I say "purely religious monasteries" because some monasteries rivalled the "big houses," being established less for purely religious purposes than for the economic exploitation of the land through the cultivation of sugar-cane by large numbers of slaves owned by monks or religious orders. Indeed, some of the powerful religious orders that took an active part in colonizing Brazil, instead of condemning the plantation regime for its un-Christian abuses, admitted it as the dominating force in colonial life and economic structure and adapted themselves to it.

Another evidence of the adaptation of the religious lords to the plantation regime and, sometimes, of recognition of its superior power, is the fact that, unlike Spanish America, Portuguese America never became noted for magnificent cathedrals. These would have symbolized powerful bishops, a powerful Church, a strong clergy. But there was never in colonial Brazil a really powerful Church or a strong clergy; nor were there domineering bishops, since each important sugar-planter, though a devout Catholic, was a sort of Philip II in regard to the Church: he considered himself more powerful than the bishops or abbots.

This explains why the plantation system and the Jesuit system were most of the time in conflict. The Jesuits did not easily admit the supremacy of the plantation system over their own. Their supreme dream in Brazil seems to have been that of a rigidly theocratic system or regime, like the "republic" they founded in Paraguay; and in such a system the "big house," with its harem and other abominations, would be a blot on a green valley. Since, however, they were unable to destroy or undermine the powerful plantation system, the Jesuits concentrated their energy on developing an educational system that would bring under their influence the rich colonists' children as well as the Indian children. In their schools, which soon became famous, white and Indian youths were taught Latin and rhetoric. Since blacks and mulattoes, however, were not usually admitted, the Jesuits are not to be accounted among the influences that favoured race amalgamation and ethnic and social democracy in Brazil. This type of democracy was a direct product of frontier life and pioneering and a by-product of the aristocratic plantation system, where miscegenation developed freely.

From what has been said of Brazil's plantation system, and of its contrasting frontier activity, a student of Anglo-American social history might conclude that the development of Portuguese America was not greatly different from that of the United States. And the fact is that a number of Brazilian tendencies and developments may be equated with the two most important systems in American industrial society, in the light of what is said of the latter by an American scholar, Professor Ulrich B. Phillips: that they form a large part of the American past from which the present with its resources, its industrial and social constitution, and its problems, has resulted. What he writes about the plantation system in the United States describes Brazilian conditions also: "The plantation system was evolved to answer the specific need of meeting the world's demand for certain staple crops in the absence of a supply of free labor. That system, providing efficient control and direction for labor imported in bondage, met the obvious needs of the case, waxed strong, and shaped not alone the industrial regime to fit its requirements, but also the social and commercial system and the political policy of a vast section."[1]

Just as Negro slavery and cotton or tobacco grew up together in the Old South of the United States, so Negro slavery and sugar and, later, coffee grew up together in that vast section of Brazil where the planters

---

1. *Plantation and Frontier, 1649–1863* (Cleveland, 1909), *Documentary History of American Industrial Society* (Cleveland, 1910), I, 71–72.

were the political lords. There, as in the United States, the one-crop system moved westward to newer land, carrying with it slavery and other institutions until, in some parts of the country (Matto Grosso, Pará, and Rio Grande do Sul), frontiers-men and planters met and developed hybrid forms of social organization. As in the United States, so in the Brazilian plantation areas more orthodox in their feudal characteristics, one-crop agriculture frequently vitiated the soil, deprived the population of food crops, and necessitated a terribly illbalanced diet.

The Brazilian frontiers-men were more obedient to the laws of tropical nature than were the planters. Though there was no refinement on the frontier, the life, though nomadic, was healthier than that of the sedentary planters. For example, some of the latter ate food procured from Portugal, in an age when food brought from Europe seldom reached Brazil in good condition.

Unlike the first generations of planters, of whom many had brought wives from Portugal and whose descendants intermarried among themselves, most of the frontiers-men of Brazil were not pure Portuguese but Portuguese-Indian hybrids: the *bandeirantes*, the *paulistas*, later the *cearenses*—descendants of Portuguese and Spaniards who had taken Indian women as their companions, and a type of pioneer that has hardly any North American counterpart except the Canadian *métis*. Because of the prominence of this type in the exploration of new areas, colonization soon ceased to be strictly

European and became a process of auto-colonization—a process that has recently become nation-wide in Brazil. Mr. Normano calls "the adjustment of existing territories to the economic life of the nation, the internal national colonization." And he seems to be right in considering this new phase of Brazilian colonization of Brazil an aspect of the phenomenon described by Turner as "the moving frontier." [2]

Judged by what they were able to accomplish, the *paulistas*, the *bandeirantes*, and the *cearenses* have been a more brilliant expression of hybrid vigour than any other to be found in America. Some time ago Professor Hooton, the American anthropologist, wrote me from Harvard that as a student of hybridization he has been enormously interested in the history of the *paulistas*. Professor Hooton is one of the leading anthropologists of our day who do not think that the notion of the physical and constitutional inferiority of the hybrid can be seriously entertained. He points out in his lectures and essays that mixtures of widely differing races produce in some instances hybrids resembling one or other of the parental stocks but more often types displaying a combination of features drawn from all the races involved in the cross. Occasionally, according to Professor Hooton and other anthropologists, the combinations blend into new and apparently stable types. This seems to have been true of the *paulistas*, as a result of the cross of Spaniards, Portuguese, and (to a very

2. J. F. Normano, *Brazil, A Study of Economic Types* (Chapel Hill, 1935), p. 2.

small extent) Negroes with Indians. They seem to have developed into a new and stable type of man or race, known for their vigour, their endurance, their fighting capacity, and the qualities or virtues of pioneers. This seems to be true also of the *cearenses* and other regional types of Brazil.

The *paulistas* first became noted for their slave-hunting expeditions—"*entradas*"—from which they brought back pure Indians as slaves for the plantations. They went over the Chaco, across the Paraguay River, as far as Bolivia. One party penetrated to the neighbourhood of Quito, on the Ecuador plateau, and a small expedition is said to have crossed the Andes.

It is easy to see why the *paulistas* came into conflict with the Jesuits, whose policy it was—in Brazil as in Canada—to segregate the Indians under a very artificial system of perpetual parental tutelage and to prevent or discourage intermarriage of whites with the natives, on the theory that "the Indian mind was incapable of high development." On this point a few modern anthropologists agree with the Jesuits: the Whethams (William Cecil Dampier and Catherine Durning), for instance, in *The Family and the Nation* (London, 1909), praise the Jesuits for their "considerable scientific insight and wisdom" as champions of racial purity in the American continent. But anthropologists who have carefully studied the problem of the American Indian and of the half-breed from a biological as well as from a social point of view—men like Boas, Dixon, Hooton, Gamio, Mendieta Nuñez, and E. Roquette Pinto—if asked to pass a judgment on the subject would probably find less "scientific insight and wisdom" in the segregation policy followed by the Jesuits than in the establishment of joint schools for natives and whites alike, which was the policy of the Portuguese Crown in Brazil and even of the Jesuits under the pressure of some of the Portuguese kings and statesmen.

The first generations of *paulistas* were not the result of any deliberate policy; they were the consequence of the scarcity of white or European women in that part of sixteenth-century Brazil. The old Lusitanian spirit celebrated by Camoëns in his famous poem took some of the most ambitious and bold Portuguese men into the jungle or the hinterland of tropical South America, where Indian women were easy and polygamy was one of the compensations for hardship. Of the typical *paulista* or *bandeirante* it has been pointed out, by more than one interpreter of his personality, that his first virtue was a resignation described by some as "almost fatalistic." Many *paulistas* or *bandeirantes* never returned from the hinterland; they remained there, multiplying themselves in mestizo children and founding towns in what were to be the provinces of Minas Geraes, Matto Grosso, Goyaz, and Bahia. Santo Amaro, for instance, was founded by a João Amaro who was for years the bravest man known in that region. For soon the *paulistas'* aim expanded from the mere capture of Indians for slavery to the conquest of the interior, the establishment of settlements and towns, the search for

FRONTIER AND PLANTATION 45

mines of gold and precious stones, and the repression of Spanish attempts at entry from the South and from Peru—a rather complex activity that has been studied by a number of Brazilian historians and geographers concentrating on the fascinating question of how Portuguese America became such a vast part of the American continent: Theodoro Sampaio, João Ribeiro, Alcantara Machado, Affonso de E. Taunay, Basilio de Magalhães, Paulo Prado, and Cassiano Ricardo.

An American author, L. E. Elliott, writes that the *bandeira*, "in its greatest phase, was a traveling city," "a commune linked by common interest";[3] and Senhor Cassiano Ricardo, who has recently written an overenthusiastic but stimulating and penetrating essay about the *bandeiras*, remarks that they, more than any other institution, promoted the ethnic and social democracy so characteristic of Brazil. While the plantation system was aristocratic in its structure—though democratic in its by-product, the mestizo, as I have said—the *bandeira* is praised by Senhor Antonio Ricardo and others of its admirers for having been thoroughly democratic. Mr. Roy Nash attempts to explain the success of those democratic "traveling cities" or "communes" by saying that the *bandeirantes*, "like the Bolsheviki," formed a militant minority which could co-operate and did not lack cohesion or social solidarity.[4] The work accomplished by the *paulistas* and by Brazilians from other regions

---

3. *Brazil: Today and Tomorrow* (New York, 1917), p. 28.
4. *The Conquest of Brazil* (New York, 1926), p. 104.

who have distinguished themselves in the history of the "moving frontier" in Brazil remains a very impressive example of the hybrid's capacity not only for action but for co-operation. In Brazil the "moving frontier" has meant the creation of ways of life and new combinations of culture—a capacity that some eloquent "Nordic" enthusiasts would like to identify exclusively with their purely white idols.

But, fascinating as were the first frontiers-men of Brazil, the *bandeirantes,* one should not forget that while they were adding vast tracts to the colony, the first generations of sugar-cane planters of the coast were not having an entirely easy task. Attacks from Indians, from English and French pirates, and especially from the Dutch disturbed the planters' agricultural routine. They had also to deal with revolts of Negro slaves, though these do not seem to have been so numerous or violent as in other areas of America, perhaps because the treatment of slaves by the Portuguese, and later by the Brazilians, was less provocative of rebellion. This is the conclusion that Brazilian students of the social history of their country have reached through what seems to be as objective and impartial a means as possible: the opinion of foreigners who knew slavery conditions in various regions of America.[5] One of these foreigners was an American missionary, the Reverend

---

5. Gilberto Freyre, "Social Life in Brazil in the Middle of the 19th Century," *The Hispanic American Historical Review,* V (1922), 597–628.

Mr. Creary, whose notes on the plantation system of Brazil were never published but remain in manuscript in the Library of Congress. His opinion is particularly valuable because it comes from a man who was a very unsympathetic critic of Brazilian customs in plantation days. Nevertheless he remarked that Brazilian slaves in the southern part of the Empire were "fairly treated and generally had much more liberty than was compatible with very efficient service." [6] As to the northern part of the Empire, Alfred Russel Wallace, the famous British scientist and abolitionist of the nineteenth century, found them generally well treated and "as happy as children." [7] And Mme. Ida Pfeiffer, who visited Brazil in the late 'forties and who was one of the most intelligent travellers of her age, wrote: "I am almost convinced that, on the whole, the lot of these slaves is less wretched than that of the peasants of Russia, Poland or Egypt, who are not called slaves." [8] But it is an English clergyman, the Reverend Hamlet Clark, who strikes the most radical note about slavery in the plantations of nineteenth-century Brazil: "Nay indeed, we need not go far to find in free England the absolute counterpart of slavery: Mayhew's London Labour and the London Poor, Dickens' Oliver Twist, Hood's Song of the Shirt and many other revelations tell of a grinding, flinty-

---

6. R. Creary, "Brazil Under the Monarchy" and "*Chronicas Lageanas*," 1886 (Ms. in Library of Congress).
7. *A Narrative of Travels on the Amazon and Rio Negro* (London, 1852), p. 120.
8. *Voyage autour du Monde* (Paris, 1868), p. 18.

hearted despotism that Brazilian slave-owners never can approach."⁹ Another traveller who knew Brazil during the full maturity of the Brazilian slave system—the first half of the nineteenth century—was W. H. B. Webster. He found the slaves of Brazil happier than most philanthropists considered them.¹⁰ An investigation of conditions of work on Brazilian plantations conducted by a British committee—a committee eager to find abuses—revealed in 1847–1848 that lenient laws were favourable to the good treatment of the slaves; that holidays, which amounted to about thirty-five days a year, were allowed them for feasting or for earning money to free themselves (manumission); that in contrast with conditions on the West Indian plantations, where slaves were hired out for profit, the typical Brazilian planter had a patriarchal feeling for his slaves. José Cliff, who appeared before that British committee (Select Committee on Coffee and Sugar Planting) said that in Brazil—a country he knew well—human nature ruled against the separation of small children from their mothers.¹¹ Koster, an English merchant who lived in northern Brazil for years, wrote that the European planter was likely to have purchased his slaves on credit, whereas the Brazilian inherited his and had nothing to urge him on to get

---

9. *Letters Home from Spain, Algeria and Brazil* (London, 1867), p. 160.
10. *Narrative of a Voyage to the South Atlantic Ocean* (London, 1834), p. 43.
11. *British Foreign and State Papers*, LXII, 622, XXXII, 126; *Reports from Committees* (House of Commons), *Session of 1847–1848*, p. 201.

greater profits;[12] and Robert Southey, in his famous *History of Brazil,* refers to the laws by which the situation of the slaves was mitigated.[13] Such evidence seems to show that the slave on Brazilian plantations was generally well treated and that his lot was really "less wretched" than that of European labourers who were not called slaves. As my old teacher in Columbia University, Professor Carlton Hayes, more than once reminded his students, audiences in England wept at hearing how cruel masters "licked" their cowering slaves in Jamaica; but in their own England little Englishmen and Englishwomen ten years old were whipped to their work—even in factories owned by the anti-slavery orators.

I have no doubt that some of the anti-slavery orators in Brazil saw in their old age, on plantations belonging to some of the modern and highly commercialized sugar factories, labour conditions much worse than those that they knew in their youth under the horrid name of slavery. Were they now living, they would probably agree with the modern students of Brazilian social history on this point: that, taken as a whole, slavery on nineteenth-century Brazilian plantations seems to have been less despotic than slavery in other American areas; and less cruel—if one admits degrees in cruelty—than the regime of labour in industrial Europe during the first terrible fifty years of economic *laissez-faire* that followed the Industrial Revolution. Less cruel, also, than

12. Henry Koster, *Travels in Brazil* (London, 1817), II, 183.
13. *History of Brazil* (London, 1822), p. 674.

the regime of labour in latter-day Brazil, where the worker's condition in fields and factories is still a problem very difficult of solution.

Of course one is always under the risk of becoming sentimental about the old days; that is, indeed, the attitude of some Brazilians in regard to the plantation system as well as to the monarchical system of government which, for nearly a century of Brazil as an independent nation, maintained the same political tradition as that under which the colony had lived from the sixteenth century to the beginning of the nineteenth. "Ideal colouring" is sometimes given by authors in Brazil, just as in the United States, to plantation life in the old days; in Brazil "ideal colouring" distorts also the picture of political conditions during the Monarchy or the Empire.

The best evidence indicates that there was much suffering in those days; that social conditions were far from being ideal; that public hygiene or sanitation was a myth. But no careful student of the subject should go so far as to dismiss entirely the legends of the Brazilian plantation and the Brazilian monarchy as nothing but sentimental or literary fancy. For both of these made possible the development of human and cultural values that remain some of the most characteristic traditions of Brazil. It would be foolish for Brazilians to desire to return to the days when those values were not only active, powerful, and exclusive. But it would be equally foolish to deny that from them the Brazilians acquired distinctive qualities—not simply a feudalistic social and psychological complex that seems to make most of the descendants of the lordly class arrogant and even sadistic and most of the descendants of slaves too unambitious and too obsequious and even childish and masochistic in their behaviour and in some of their attitudes.

One should never forget, however, that neither the plantation system nor the monarchical system ever meant, in Brazil, hard social gradations; it was possible for men of exceptional talent, no matter how socially inferior their origin, to rise to the highest positions in the Brazilian aristocratic and monarchical system. And it was customary for plantation lords to have their illegitimate brown children, when brilliant, as well educated as the legitimate ones. Webster observed that in nineteenth-century Brazil some of the most intelligent Negroes owned by kind masters were educated with the masters' children and that some attained great success after their liberation.[14] This means that in Brazil neither the plantation system nor the monarchical system was rigidly closed to social or political democracy; the present anti-democratic tendency is a very recent development and is contrary not only to our republican avowals but to our monarchical and plantation traditions. Each of the traditions, taken as a whole, was a combination of democratic and aristocratic tendencies rather than a pure expression of immoderately despotic, autocratic, dictatorial trends. Such trends were possibly more characteristic of some of the Spanish American republics in their *caudillo* phases than of monarchical

14. *Op. cit.*, p. 43.

and aristocratic Brazil, where the plantation system acted as a powerful republican opposition to any autocratic excess on the part of the Crown and where the Crown served as a permanent limit to autocratic excesses on the part of plantation lords. The result was that Brazil developed a healthier democratic (or pre-democratic) condition from the rivalry between almost equal powers, which neutralized—yet respected—each other, than did the Spanish American republics in which, under the name of Presidents, *caudillos* and dictators, generals and adventurers were able to exercise absolute power during years and years of sometimes sadistic rule.

I do not mean to belittle the Spanish American republics that have had *caudillos*, or to over-praise Brazil for the fact that a monarchy, combined with an aristocratic plantation system, prevented Portuguese America from having *caudillismo*. For some of those Spanish American republics have a right to laugh at Brazil—a Brazil that knew no real *caudillos* during the nineteenth century but has known *caudillismo* since the Republic was established there in 1889: Pinheiro Machado, for instance, was a *caudillo* and a very recent one. Even during the monarchical days Brazil, exceptionally it is true, had a de-luxe *caudillo* as prime minister; though he wore a frock coat and not a military uniform and made no attempt to close the Imperial Parliament, he was intolerant of political differences and reduced the political parties to insignificant groups. I refer to the Marquis of Paraná, who was more imperial in his activities than the Emperor himself. But he was an exception, and, though an autocrat, a very elegant one; he was not an ordinary *caudillo*.

As a rule, the leaders of the Brazilian government during the Monarchy came from the oldest plantation areas—Bahia, Pernambuco, São Paulo, Rio de Janeiro—and some of them were statesmen, not mere politicians. Some became champions of great democratic reforms: Joaquim Nabuco, for instance. More than once, popular opinion expressed itself through them. This is what makes me say that, though it sounds like a paradox, one finds in monarchical and aristocratic Brazil as it was during the great days of the plantation regime a healthier pre-democratic condition than in some of the nineteenth-century Spanish American republics dominated by *caudillos* and harassed by revolutions.

The student of the Brazilian plantation system is tempted to compare it with the plantation system in other areas of America, especially the South of the United States. The system in Anglo-Saxon America probably had a more rigid aristocratic structure, from the point of view of race superiority and inferiority, than in Brazil, where race prejudice was never so strong as among Anglo-Saxons. There was race prejudice among plantation-area Brazilians; there was social distance between master and slave, between white and black, just as between old and young, man and woman. But few Brazilian aristocrats were so strict about racial purity as the majority of the Anglo-American aristocrats of the Old South were. Family pride was stronger than race pride. And women were probably more oppressed by men in the Brazilian system than in the Old South. There were, however, exceptions; occasionally women were the heads of the houses or plantations. My grandfather knew one when he was a young boy. Her name was Dona Felicia and her slaves, her children, and also her husband were known as Dona Felicia's slaves, children, and husband. She carried a whip with her to punish children, slaves, and even her husband. But such situations were exceptional.

The elements that composed the plantation ensemble in Brazil were practically the same as those that characterized the plantation ensemble in the United States; plantation cooking is certainly one of them. The "trinity of figures" suggested by former Governor Taylor of Tennessee for a monument to the Old South of the United States might be used by a Brazilian sculptor for a similar monument to the old North of Brazil. And instead of being restricted to a regional glorification, the idea might indeed be expanded to a glorification of the "Old Plantation" on the American continent, to embrace not only the North of Brazil, but also other areas or regions of the Hispanic, Anglo-Saxon, French, and Dutch Americas. For such "a trinity of figures" as the one suggested by Governor Taylor—consisting of "the courtly old planter, high bred and gentle in face and manner"; "the plantation uncle, the counterpart in ebony of the master so loyally served," and "the broad-bosomed black mammy with vari-colored turban, spotless apron and beaming face, the friend of every living

Frontier and Plantation

thing in cabin or mansion"—corresponds to a tradition common to all aristocratic plantation areas of America. There may be over-simplification, besides an excessive idealization of the past, in Governor Taylor's idea for this monument, since the plantation system in America was a complex one and its harsh aspects were probably as numerous as its pleasant. But the "trinity of figures" existed—in Brazil as well as in the Old South of the United States.

Professor Francis Pendleton Gaines in his book *The Southern Plantation*, published in New York in 1925— three years after the publication of my first attempt to characterize the Brazilian plantation—mentions other equally important types of the Southern system or complex: "the gay girl from Dixie"; "the young cavalier"; "the prototype of Negro minstrelsy."[15] Professor Thompson mentions "the driver";[16] Professor Cotteril refers to "the overseer universally detested by the slaves."[17] All these personality and social types established by the "isolation of plantation life" existed in Brazil. From a Brazilian point of view, I should like to see included in a monument to the Plantation the plantation mistress; the field slave; the *muleque*, or Negro boy, who was the white boy's patient and sometimes masochistic companion; and the mulatto young woman who had in Brazil the African name of *mucama*: "the

---

15. P. 15.
16. Edgar T. Thompson, "The Plantation: the Physical Basis of Traditional Race Relations," in *Race Relations and the Race Problem* (Durham, 1939), p. 214.
17. R. S. Cotteril, *The Old South* (Glendale, 1939), p. 268.

white mistress's companion." Such a monument would perhaps become too crowded to be an effective glorification of heroes of the past—though according to some architects and social philosophers this is what most monuments should be: the glorification of groups and not of individual heroes.

As in the South of the United States, so in Brazil not all plantation masters were "courtly," "high bred," and "gentle in face and manner." The distinction established in this country by Professor Gaines's scholarly essay referred to above—the distinction between the Southern plantation as it appears in legend and as it really was—is one that should be made also in relation to the plantation area of Brazil; its literary apologists paint its past as too rosy. As I have suggested in one of my essays on the rural part of Brazil, not all plantation houses, but only a minority of them, were really mansions from an architectural point of view, or places where good and abundant food was the rule instead of the exception; not all sugar-cane planters were honest and noble—some mixed ordinary sand with their sugar, some were heavy drinkers, not of fine or old wines, but of ordinary rum, or *cachaça;* not a few were gamblers, and some were always in debt and as ignorant of business detail, amount of income, and number of slaves as was Colonel Dangerfield, the hero of James K. Paulding's *Westward Ho!* As for the sons of the great families, not all of them became statesmen, orators, authors, bishops, generals, or admirals; a number reached old age with no higher interest than a passion for horses, Negro women, and cock-fighting. In the plantation area of Brazil, as in the South of the United States, informal horse-racing was not a mere sport but an almost religious institution. Hunting was another. And as in the South of this country as described by Phillips, Gaines, and Thompson, so in the Brazilian plantation area the economic basis of feudal social life was precarious or uncertain. There, as here, the prevailing economic condition among slavery-age planters, first of sugar, later of coffee, was characterized by extravagance, despoiling of soil fertility, ignorance of scientific methods in agriculture, and ineffective labour; a condition that there, as in the Old South, culminated frequently in what Professor Gaines calls "bankruptcy with the break-up of an estate and sometimes westward migration." In Brazil, what ordinarily happened when a man lost his plantation was that he went to one of the sea-coast towns, where he would live a commonplace life as a secondary public employee. Sons of once very wealthy planters became lawyers, judges, and doctors in frontier towns.

Festive occasions drew together many rural families in the plantation area. Saint John's Eve, in June, was probably the greatest day of the year on Brazilian sugarcane plantations, at least on the oldest and most typical of them. There were European dances in the interior of the mansions, where silver—a common luxury—and shining glass appeared in all their glory, while outside, the Negroes danced their African dances, especially the samba, around large bonfires built to honour Saint John and to keep the Devil away. Food was abundant.

Special cakes, particularly of corn, were made for the occasion. As a feast day Saint John's Eve was the Brazilian equivalent of Christmas on the Southern plantations.

One of the Portuguese traditions connected with Saint John's Eve as celebrated in old Brazil was that of bathing and washing: one should take a special bath. I say a special bath because Brazilians have always been fond of baths: sometimes more than one a day, as nineteenth-century European travellers noticed in the plantation area. Warren, an American who was in Brazil in the middle of the last century, says that on his landing there the first spectacle that arrested his attention was that of a number of persons of both sexes and all ages—persons of the common people—bathing in the waters of a river. He observed among them "several finely formed Indian girls of exceeding beauty dashing about in the water like a troop of happy mermaids." [18] The aristocrats were not so pagan; they had private baths constructed of palms in rivers that were almost private rivers, almost private plantation property. And there the ladies bathed daily, swimming also like happy mermaids. For swimming was one of the characteristic sports of the plantation area.

Wedding days were also among the great feast days of plantation life in Brazil, just as in the Old South of the United States. But to weddings one should add, in

---

18. John Esaias Warren, *Pará; or Scenes and Adventures on the Banks of the Amazon* (New York, 1851), p. 9. See also Freyre, "Social Life in Brazil in the Middle of the 19th Century," p. 626.

regard to Brazil, the days when white children were baptized and the day of the year when one's sugar-mill began to operate. For the latter it was the custom to have an important religious and social celebration; then the plantation chaplain or an outside priest or friar would sprinkle with holy water the first sugar-canes to be crushed in the mill.

Hospitality was customary. It is probable that in Brazil, as in the South of the United States, the pride of the big planters in keeping a good table where travellers were generously fed was not only an expression of "conspicuous waste" of the type so well described by Professor Veblen but also a manifestation of the so-called gregarious instinct intensified by isolation. Visitors of all kinds had a right to sit at the table of a plantation lord or baron and to occupy a bed in one of his guest rooms. A peculiar personality type developed in Brazil under such an excess of generous entertainment was that of the *"papa-pirão"*; that is, men who went from one plantation to another, being regaled with everything that each afforded and doing nothing but gossip, smoke cigars, and play cards. There were parasites of this type who ceased to be absolute parasites; they were also jesters or men famous for their humour, jokes, and anecdotes. Some Brazilian planters, like kings of the past, had their own private jesters or jockeys; some maintained clowns and acrobats, besides a plantation band of Negro boys.

An institution of Brazil's plantation system for which I find no equivalent in the South of the United States is the private chaplain. He was a member of the patriarchal family, with the rank of a bachelor uncle or an old and widowed grandfather, rather than that of a priest rigidly under the control of his bishop. He was under the direction of the planter, who sometimes paid him generously for his good services. He not only took care of the religious or devotional activities of whites and slaves but was also the private tutor of the boys, the one who taught them grammar, Latin, and sacred history and prepared them to enter military or naval school (or simply the army or the navy), law school, seminary, or medical school. Under the Brazilian patriarchal system, these were gentlemen's careers: the army or the navy, government, diplomacy, public administration or law, the Church or priesthood and, for the most progressive, medicine. Stimulated by the Emperor, the Imperial Academy of Medicine became a school that bestowed as much social prestige with the degrees it gave as did the two traditional law schools, Recife and São Paulo. Every generation in a family had to have a priest; it was almost a social disgrace not to have one. As families then were large—ten, twelve, even fifteen children to a single mother, or twenty or more when the aristocrat married more than once, as often happened—it was not uncommon for parents to have at least one boy who was really inclined to enter the priesthood or to be a monk in one of the many monasteries. But, if no one of the children was born with this inclination, the youngest son was sometimes made a priest or a monk against his will. This explains the large number of priests and monks in patriarchal Brazil who had no predilection for the priesthood or the monastery. The situation was not so much the fault of the Church, which accepted such entrants in order to maintain a clergy made up of sons of the aristocracy, as the consequence of the aristocratic plantation system.

Though families are not so large today among descendants of the old plantation or aristocratic stock as they were during the slavery period, they continue to be big. An American sociologist recently concluded, through a study of vital statistics, that in Brazil the trend in family size "is exactly opposite to the trend generally reported in the United States and Western Europe. The families of the well-to-do and educated are substantially larger than those in lower levels." [19] According to the same investigator, not only the number of living children of the typical planter in the State of Minas Geraes is nearly double the number of the common labourer's (the chief cause being the higher mortality rate of children in the poorer class), but the rate of fecundity of Brazilian mothers is very high. One point should be made clear: the large number of priests and monks from well-to-do plantation stock did not always mean that they were childless; some had children, and more than one prominent Brazilian has been the illegitimate descendant of a priest or a monk.

19. John B. Griffing, "A Comparison of the Effects of Certain Socioeconomic Factors upon Size of Family in China, Southern California, and Brazil" (dissertation); "Natural Eugenics in Brazil," *Journal of Heredity*, XXXI (1940), 13-16.

It was only in the latter part of the nineteenth century that there was a diminution in the sacrifice of youth, not so much to organized religion as to an organized patriarchal regime that had both youth and religion under its control. Nevertheless, the inclination of Brazilians towards those careers long considered the only decent or proper ones for gentlemen—government, diplomacy, law, public administration, medicine, priesthood, army or navy—is still to be found as a survival of the plantation system. Not only decadent aristocrats or decadent descendants of aristocrats but social upstarts eager to imitate the decadent aristocracy have followed that tradition until recently or are still following it. The reaction against the tendency is now strong but is not winning an easy victory against such deep prejudices. There seems to be no doubt that the plantation system in Brazil, with its whole structure based on slave work, developed in many Brazilians a peculiarly aristocratic attitude towards manual labour and also towards trade, business, and commercial or industrial activity. This explains, to a certain extent, why the Portuguese peasant became in Brazil the successful grocer; the Frenchman, the fancy-goods dealer; the Englishman, and later the German and the American, the wholesale importer, the engineer, the expert in industrial and mechanical work, in railroad construction, and in transportation; the Italian, the German, other Europeans, and the Japanese, the successful farmer; whereas the Brazilians of the old stocks (and those who are not of the old stocks but find it elegant or convenient to imitate them) remain, as bachelors of arts or doctors of law, of philosophy, or of medicine, a sort of bureaucratic or intellectual caste whose hands are too delicate for ignoble work and who are altogether too superior to compete with materialistic foreigners. This gentleman-complex is considered by some observers to be one of the most harmful survivals of the plantation system in Brazil. Feeling themselves above all the drudgery of life, a number of Brazilians have sought in lottery, gambling, expensive card-playing, and adventure a substitute for work. Card-playing was intimately connected with the plantation system of Brazil—as I conclude, from what I have read about the plantation system in the South of the United States, it was also in this country. Not many years ago I found a document in a Brazilian archive that seems to indicate that the first thing printed in Brazil, in colonial days, was not a newspaper or a book but a set of playing cards.

There were bullfights in colonial Brazil, but they never became so important in Brazil as in Mexico or Ecuador. Perhaps rich planters thought too much of their horses, if not of their cattle, to let them die in bullfights. For Brazilian planters, just like Southern planters in this country, were especially fond of horses. The well-to-do were almost as proud of the number of fine horses they owned as of the number of their children, legitimate and illegitimate, and of their slaves, field and domestic. Some of them were such lovers of riding that they learned to perform acrobatic stunts on horseback. Others were too lazy or too dignified even for that; when they travelled, they were carried by their Negroes in hammocks or palanquins just like Hindu princes.

There were two other points of similarity between this regime and that of the Old South in the United States—the prevalent swearing, by the masters, and their excessive individualism. What Colonel Allston said of Southern planters—that "they were the least given to acting together in combination"—might be said of Brazilian sugar-cane lords and even of coffee-planters, though the latter eventually learned to co-operate.

As to the effect of the plantation on intellectual life, it seems that the Brazilian system, perhaps because it was more powerful, surpassed that of the Old South in producing talented authors and scholars, besides statesmen, orators, and diplomats. The best dictionary produced in Brazil was written by a plantation master, and early in the sixteenth century an ethnological treatise was composed in Bahia by another. The Brazilian mother of Thomas Mann came from the plantation area. A number of Brazilian poets, essayists, and artists were born on plantations. As in the Old South, many mansions could show creditable libraries and some planters sent their boys to study in Europe.

There was a time when students emphasized the bad effects of the whites' contact with Negroes on the plantations, and slavery did undoubtedly stimulate, in the whites most directly touched by it, a despotic individualism as well as indolence and an aversion to manual labour. On the other hand, Brazilian culture was deeply enriched through the association of white boys with old Negro men and women who told them stories full of a humanity and sweetness that sometimes surpassed the humanity and the sweetness of the stories found in conventional school books. Slavery afforded to the ruling class a leisure that enabled a number of its talented men to study the best methods of destroying feudalism and developing democracy in Brazil—a democracy based on a knowledge of the so-called biological superiorities and inferiorities of race or class. Some of the men who have become real democratic forces in Brazilian life and art—men like Joaquim Nabuco and Sylvio Romero and, today, José Lins do Rego and Cicero Dias—have been the products of the old plantation system. Every one of them seems to know how true for Brazil are the remarks of Phillips concerning the plantation system in this country: in the plantation system there was "little of the curse of impersonality and indifference which too commonly prevails in factories of the present-day world where power-driven machinery sets the pace, where the employers have no relations with the employed outside of work hours." [20] Strange as it seems, most of the despots, *caudillos,* and anti-democratic leaders that Brazil has had did not derive from its plantation area but came from other sections.

20. U. B. Phillips, *American Negro Slavery* (New York, London, 1918), p. 307.

III

BRAZILIAN UNITY AND BRAZILIAN REGIONAL DIVERSITY

Professor Glenn R. Morrow, of the University of Pennsylvania, not long ago pointed out that the first Congress of Regionalism in Brazil—perhaps the first in America—met in Recife in 1925. Recently, at Yale University, the subject of Brazilian Regionalism was discussed at the Inter-American Conference of Philosophy, where I fear that it was not entirely understood by some members, though all comments were sympathetic and generous. Regionalism, as understood and described by Brazilian regionalists, is a social philosophy; and one of the main objections voiced at the Conference was that philosophy, being "a work of reason," cannot "accept regional data, forms of thought and of sentiment of local content, unless it corrupts and destroys itself." The view was therefore advanced by one critic that as regionalists my friends and I put too much emphasis on the regional aspect of Brazilian culture.[1]

Before attempting to discuss the two antagonisms of Brazilian life and culture—unity and regional diversity,

---

1. Afranio Continho, "Some Considerations on the Problem of Philosophy in Brazil," *Philosophy and Phenomenological Research* (1943), IV, 191.

or unitarism and regionalism—I wish to make as clear as possible the idea of regionalism as understood by modern Brazilian regionalists. They distinguish regionalism from nationalism and also from mere sectionalism —to use Professor Turner's word for sterile or self-sufficient regionalism. A region may be politically less than a nation. But vitally and culturally it is more than a nation; it is more basic both as a condition of life and as a medium of expression or creativeness. To be a genuine philosopher a man has to be super- or supra-national; but he can hardly be supra-regional in the sense of ignoring the regional condition of the life, the experience, the culture, the art, and the thought that he is considering or analyzing. As Mr. Joseph E. Baker writes in his analysis of regionalism: "The regionalist who ignores the universal is at fault, of course; the life of his region is his medium of expression, not his message, and he should not make his thinking a mere search for the curious, the odd, and the picturesque—that was the error of the local-colorist. But the internationalists (to which, indeed, our present brand of nationalism must be referred) recommend to us a literature which gives neither the universal ideal of humanity at its best, nor the subtle essence of a local culture; but rather those elementary physical and economic interests which are common to man at his crudest in Atlanta, Manchester, and Hamburg—the lowest common denominator, not the profoundest human potentialities. We are much more likely to rise to a conception of man as fully human by contemplating his achievements as they flower in different regions—of America, and of Europe." [2]

The regional point of view, considered as an approach to the study of history or sociology, seems to some of us Brazilian regionalists as philosophical as any other. This is also the conclusion reached by a South African student of regionalism, Professor Bews. He defines regionalism—under the name of "human ecology"—as "a special way of regarding the ultimate reality of life"; as a "philosophy of life," [3] and not merely as a science or a technique. One may object to Professor Bews's philosophical regionalism by saying that a strictly regional "philosophy of life" has a tendency to be incomplete. But it is a philosophy; it is a philosophical attitude or point of view. It is perhaps incomplete without its antagonistic point of view: universalism or cosmopolitanism. I agree with those who think that these two currents of thought—by some called localism and internationalism—mutually enrich each other. I agree with those who expand to the cultural sphere the well-known idea of Professor Bonn concerning economic life—the idea that there is a process of counter-colonization, as opposed to that of colonization.

It is as counter-colonization that regionalism seems to us Brazilian regionalists to be a healthy tendency in Brazilian as well as in continental American life, a tendency opposed to excessive national, as well as to exaggerated international or cosmopolitan, tendencies. But

2. "Regionalism: Pro and Con. Four Arguments for Regionalism," *Saturday Review of Literature*, XV (1936), 14.
3. J. W. Bews, *Human Ecology* (London, 1935), p. 284.

UNITY AND DIVERSITY

the three types of cultural influence—the indigenous or regional, the national (probably the most transitory and artificial of all), and the supra-national, or cosmopolitan—enrich each other; and the ideal is apparently to secure, through a combination of the three, the constant and stimulating interaction of all their antagonisms. As a political scientist wrote recently: "The principal task of the student of international organization is not to waste more time debating over regionalism versus universalism, but to study the ways in which, in concrete cases, the two principles can be utilized in combination and the standards to be applied in the dosage of each to be adopted."[4]

Some students of the social international situation that has developed in the world since the Industrial Revolution in Europe—industrial world-conquest based on ideals of standardization of all places according to the standards of the most powerful capitalistic states—have recognized the need for a creative regionalism in opposition to the many excesses of political centralization and unification of culture stimulated by politically and economically imperial interests and forces. It is the basic theory of such students that a growing number of separate cultural units will contribute to the stability of the world by preventing the formation and the expansion of imperialisms and of empires.[5] The regional-

4. Pitman B. Potter, "Universalism Versus Regionalism in International Reorganization," *The American Political Science Review*, XXXVI (1943), 862.
5. Quincy Wright, *A Study of War* (Chicago, 1942), II, pp. 1334-5.

ist movement that a group of authors, artists, and scientists started in Brazil twenty-two years ago and that was perhaps the first systematic movement of its kind in America was and continues to be an effort to encourage a more spontaneous cultural life in Brazil through a freer expression of culture by the people of the various regions. The North-east, where the movement started, is a region with a particularly rich history and is noted for its human potentiality. That region was losing consciousness of the values of its history as well as of its possibilities; the loss was occurring not only because of general standardizing influences originating in industrial world-conquest but also because of similar influences originating inside the American continent and within the Brazilian nation itself.

The danger of cultural monotony or excessive unification of culture within the American continent sprang from the influence of North American capitalistic industrialism, largely dominated by the idea that what is good for North Americans should be good for every other people of America. Some of the American manufacturers, inclined toward world uniformity, would repeat, with probably the best intentions, the same excess in that direction as was manifested by those British manufacturers who were the first to take control of the Brazilian colonial or semi-colonial market early in the nineteenth century. We are told by an Englishman [6] that so avid was the speculating in England then as

---

6. R. Walsh, *Notices of Brazil in 1828 and 1829* (Boston, 1831), I, pp. 245-246.

Unity and Diversity 71

regards the South American markets that everything was sent to Brazil, with no consideration for the fitness or adaptability of English products to the climate or to the wants of the Brazilians. Implements useful only for Europeans, comforts and conveniences fit only for Britons, Scandinavians, Russians, Germans, and inhabitants of the Alps, were sent in abundance to tropical Brazil—warm blankets, warming-pans to heat them, and even ice skates. True, most of the blankets were adapted by the Brazilians to the purpose of gold-washing in the rivers of the Minas Geraes region; most of the warming-pans were used in the sugar-mills of the North-east regions; and even the skates were turned to a new use: wrought iron for shoeing mules and horses being scarce in Brazil then, the more intelligent Brazilians altered the British skates and put them on their horses' feet. But I have no doubt that a few of the most colonial-minded actually tried themselves to use the blankets, the warming-pans, and the skates, so as to look European, Nordic, or civilized.

I have known a number of Brazilian ladies who in Brazil wear such furs as are fashionable on winter days in Paris, London, and New York; and a number of wealthy Brazilian men have built themselves residences, not fitted to the tropical or near-tropical conditions of most of the country, but designed in rigid Scandinavian, Dutch, or Norman style. And more than once Brazil has copied its constitutions so closely from European ones or from that of the United States that the Brazilian political situation has been as artificial, as ridiculous, and as absurd as the use by a tropical people of ice skates in order to appear as civilized or fashionable as the Swiss, the Scandinavian, or the British.

The sending of ice skates and furs to Brazil by European or American manufacturers—whose ideal world would be one in which every people would have a polar or near-polar winter with plenty of ice for the universal use of skates and furs, to the benefit of large-scale industrial production—illustrates the ideal and the interest of manufacturers of goods and ideas who think in imperial terms. For them the world is divided into two areas: the imperial area, where goods and ideas are manufactured according to the manufacturers' needs and regional culture standards; and the colonial area, where people are expected to live, not according to their own needs and regional conditions, but according to standards imposed on them by those manufacturers. It is a reaction against this type of cosmopolitan standardization based on an almost divine right of colonization of areas technically less advanced by peoples who happen to be the most powerful ones from a technical and military point of view, that a movement directed towards counter-colonization has been developing among nations, regions, or populations whose cultures are the most diverse—the Mexicans, the Arabs, the East Indians, the Brazilians, to mention only a few—but whose "consciousness of kind" (to use Giddings's expression) is the same: they all feel that their colonial or semi-colonial status is doing harm to their creative capacity and their human potentiality. Under such a status they have become pure imitators, instead of creators of culture. And as Professor John Dewey says: "Since we can neither beg nor borrow a culture without betraying both it and ourselves, nothing remains save to produce one."

The problem of Brazil as a culturally creative nation has been not only the problem of resisting outside imperialistic attempts to maintain as cultural colonies countries like those of Latin America under various pretexts and so-called reasons or needs for strict unity or unification—as a Pan-American unity sometimes used for the sole benefit of the United States or a Hispanic unity meant to be an instrument of domination by Spain over its former colonies of America. It also has been and is the problem of combining sub-regional diversity with national unity.

Ecologically Brazil is a region, to a large extent a natural region—so clearly so that it is considered by some geographers a "continental island." It is also a cultural region, a population whose predominating cultural values and standards are of Portuguese origin, in contrast to the Spanish, Dutch, English, and French values and standards of its American neighbours.

But Brazil is not simply one natural and cultural region; inside the almost continental immensity of that part of America, Nature and culture have their own subdivisions. Therefore Brazil needs to defend itself permanently against its own enemies of its organic regionalism. For Brazil has more than once in its history had leaders whose ideal or whose mystical conception of a Brazilian Nation or Empire or Power has been that of Philip II in regard to Spain: the absolute supremacy of some Castile—I use the name Castile as a symbol of the tendency to over-emphasize unity over diversity—over the other regions of the country.

Castilianism in Brazil, as I see it, has not meant only a region striving, through some Philip II, to dominate the other regions. Nor has it been only a State—technically a Federal State with no more rights than any other, but actually an imperial power—striving to dominate the remaining States. This happened during the first Republican period of Brazil: more than once a State—an almost entirely artificial political State—dominated the other States of the Union through quite mechanical or quantitative advantages, such as a larger number, not so much of people as of voters or votes, and through a larger number of banks, factories, and manufactures.

Castilianism in Brazil—again as I see it—may mean and has meant other forms of domination by brutally powerful majorities over minorities whose rights should be respected to a larger extent than those majorities are willing to admit—that is, if we are to have really creative cultural diversity instead of a mere imitation of it. It may mean and has meant other forms of domination by technically powerful minorities over abused or exploited majorities. An example of the first type would be the excessive zeal of certain members of the vast Portuguese or Luso-Brazilian majority for the cultural uniformity or unity of Brazil so far as Portuguese or

Unity and Diversity

Luso-Brazilian values are concerned; they consider a menace to Brazilian unity any opportunity for creative expression given to non-Portuguese European groups or to non-European or mixed groups. Of course, here we are not concerned with inter-regional antagonisms of a strictly geographical configuration, but with inter-regional antagonisms or conflict in social and cultural realms rather than in physical space. Most of the Brazilian cultural sub-regions, however, have natural or physical sub-regions as their main bases: the purely white minority of Brazil, for instance, is located more in the South than in the North. That is also true of the non-Portuguese or non-Luso Brazilians; their "sub-regions" are more in the extreme southern part of Brazil than in any part of the North.

Obviously a healthy minimum of cultural basic uniformity is necessary if Brazil is to remain a confederation instead of becoming a vast boarding-house—the "boarding-house" of Theodore Roosevelt's famous metaphor in regard to the United States. And that minimum is traditionally composed, in Brazil, of Luso or Hispanic basic values and cultural means of inter-regional and inter-human communication. The most important of these means is the Portuguese language. That minimum is made also of values and even techniques predominantly European, and not Amerindian or African—predominantly but not exclusively.

The entire subordination of historical and geographical differences to a rigid ideal of uniformity would be too narrow an ideal of unity for such a complex cultural "continent" as Brazil. Over-simplification of the problem of Brazilian complexity through its subordination to mere political convenience was one of the weaknesses of the Empire in Brazil, noted for its excess of centralization. Some students of Brazilian problems think that it is one of the defects of the present political regime. That regime has gone too far in its reaction against the excess, not of creative regionalism, but of "state rights" developed in Portuguese America during the so-called "first Republic." "State rights" was one of the Anglo-American political theories imported by Brazilian republicans from the United States without a previous careful study of Brazilian geographical and historical conditions. The result was that national parties almost ceased to exist in Brazil; populous and powerful rival States like São Paulo, Minas Geraes, and Rio Grande do Sul developed into something like political parties. Each one of them had as its real political program not so much the solution of national, or Brazilian, problems of social and human interest as the promotion of narrowly sectional or state interests, industrial, commercial, and agricultural. There was a railroad built in one of the powerful States, with Federal or national money, that was an almost luxurious enterprise for Brazil—most of it with double track—while there were Brazilian regions in which transportation needs were entirely neglected. Descendants of Germans were allowed liberties or privileges entirely incompatible with Brazilian cultural basic unity (such as the right to have schools where Portuguese was not

Unity and Diversity

taught) by politicians who needed German votes in order to dominate or control their particular State. Other politicians were interested in making of their particular State the economic Castile or the political and even military Prussia of Brazil—power politics within the national sphere. There was a time when the police force of the State São Paulo was nearly as powerful as the Brazilian Army. It had its own French military instructors and other features characteristic of a national army. The same, or almost the same thing, has happened in Rio Grande do Sul and in Minas Geraes. I once came from Minas Geraes with the vivid impression that I had been in a Brazilian Prussia. A vast amount of public money was being spent, not on public works or for the permanent benefit of the people, but to maintain a police force almost as powerful as the national army. What for? Apparently for the defence of state rights—really, perhaps, for the defence of a political group that was then in power in that particular State. Whatever the reason, the fact was not an expression of healthy or creative regionalism but a horrid caricature of it. American students of the problem of regionalism are right when they establish a fundamental distinction between regionalism and sectionalism. Some of the pages written by Turner about sectionalism in the United States might have been written about the same problem in Brazil.

At present, under a regime that some describe as an "authoritarian democracy," the prevailing *mystique* (to use the French word) in Brazil—that is, the *mystique* that official propaganda emphasizes through its radios and newspapers as the only basis for orthodox patriotism—is the opposite extreme of the doctrine of "state rights" as it was known from 1889 to 1930. It is the dangerous *mystique* of Castilian unity or Castilian uniformity. "Castilian" in this case does not mean, as it did in old Spain, the supremacy of one Brazilian region over the others. It means centralization: political centralization. It means the excessive subordination of a country as vast as Brazil to its political capital: to Rio.

One cannot deny that Senhor Getulio Vargas and other "unionists" or "centralists" have done away with excesses or abuses of "state rights." For the fact is that the 1889 Republic in Brazil was marked by "a tariff war between the states—between them and the Union." [7] But some have reached an extreme point in their ideal or their policy of political centralization and national uniformity—a point at which the cure may do more harm to the politically sick nation than the disease. The disease was an excess of state rights, so prominent and harmful in Brazil before the 1930 Revolution. The cure is the present excess of uniformity, with the central power directing everything in Brazil. There are exceptions: States like Pernambuco have since 1937 been almost independent from Rio in the semi-Fascist or para-Fascist characteristics that they have developed. Such exceptions show that the modern regime needs modification, not only for the sake of a freer local life, but also for the sake of a more effective control of national affairs

7. J. F. Normano, *op. cit.*, p. 123.

UNITY AND DIVERSITY

by a vigilant, independent, and critical public opinion and press.

"Unionism" or "centralism" is not an innovation in Brazil. The Brazilian Empire, as I said, was noted for centralization. That was one of its defects. But it did probably less harm to Brazilian regional and cultural diversity than the present system of centralization and uniformity is doing. For during the Empire centralized power was in the hands, not only of a constitutional emperor whose abuses, or attempts at abuse, of centralized power were sharply criticized in Parliament and in a free press, but also of the intellectually and morally best and ablest public-minded men of Brazil. Most of these reached supreme power after having given public evidence, in their own provinces, of their capacity and honesty, and not (like most of them today) through a strictly personal choice by the President or chief of the nation. Some of them rose to power from very humble origin. At least two of them—Rebouças and Saldanha Marinho—were almost jet-black and of slave descent; and several were mulattoes, the descendants of slaves. For the Empire in Brazil was remarkable for its combination of politically aristocratic methods with ways and customs as democratic as those of any republic that the continent has had. It was remarkable for its tendency towards an ethnic and social democracy—not only a remote Brazilian tradition but a Portuguese tradition as well. I shall later stress this tradition as a characteristic of Brazilian social and cultural development.

The men who founded the Federal Republic that in 1889 replaced the Empire had been impressed by the excesses of centralized power in their vast country. They adopted a constitution that copied that of the United States. Instead of seeking to combine unity with regional diversity, they borrowed from the United States the principle of "state rights," thus putting such an emphasis on a political state autonomy derived from merely quantitative conditions and advantages held by one state over the others that many abuses became possible. The problem of combining diversity with unity —perhaps the most fundamental problem in organizing Brazil as a community—seems to have suffered as much from the political methods of combining them adopted by the Federal Republic of 1889 as from the centralization methods followed by the Empire. The solution of the problem appears to be not a narrowly political one, but a social one, whereby states are reduced to a minimum of importance and natural and cultural regions are treated as organic realities, each with its own characteristics but all vitally interdependent in their economic interests and needs; all vitally interdependent for the solution of their social and cultural problems and aspirations. Diversity will then become creative as never before; and unity will be less of a problem than now, with regions co-ordinated by an inter-regional organism but not oppressed or exploited by the region or sectional group economically or technically most powerful at the moment.

UNITY AND DIVERSITY

It seems to some of us, as students of regionalism, that countries with a regional past, like Brazil, ought to keep constantly in mind the example of Spain, where centuries of systematic Castilianization did not succeed in imposing Castilian regional culture on all Hispanic regions as their only or sacred culture. From the point of view of unity, Brazilians are fortunate in having a single language—the Portuguese. Differences of pronunciation have never been significant in Portuguese-speaking America, though a Congress met recently in São Paulo—a *paulista* initiative, not one of the central government of Rio—at which some of the best philologists, authors, composers, musicians, historians, and sociologists of Brazil were present to study the problem of the Portuguese language in Brazil. There it was decided that the Portuguese spoken in Rio by the so-called *carioca* (the inhabitant of the capital of Brazil) is the most agreeable to the ear and the best adapted to music, to song, to the theatre, to the cinema, and to public speaking. Its adoption as the Portuguese to be used by composers, dramatists, and professional public speakers was a unanimous decision of the São Paulo Congress and was well received by all Brazilians. This does not mean that regional linguistic peculiarities are to be avoided by writers, or in the theatre, the song, and the drama when regional characters appear: far from it. It means that one of the Brazilian regional ways of pronouncing the Portuguese language—the *carioca* way—has been chosen by a very representative group of

Brazilians as the official language for the Brazilian theatre, Brazilian song, and the Brazilian cinema when regional characters do not appear in them.

So reasonable and sensible a measure is a good example of the possibilities of combining unity with diversity in a country almost continental in its extension. And a significant thing about it is that it came from São Paulo—a sort of Catalonia of Brazil: a manufacturing region that has no equal in Latin America, with a capital that is the most European and at the same time the most "Yankee" of the Brazilian cities, and a people whose cult of efficiency and love of toil are in sharp contrast to the almost Chinese indifference and resignation to poverty of certain Brazilian groups of other regions. Like the Catalans of Spain, some *paulistas* feel that their industry is helping to maintain others in idleness; one *paulista* has compared São Paulo to a locomotive pulling the rest of Brazil, twenty mere cars —possibly sleeping cars. But, also like the Catalans, *paulistas* tend to become proud, arrogant, and even prone to exaggerate when they contrast their brilliant economic achievements with those of Brazilian Andalusians: Brazilians from Bahia, Pernambuco, and Rio Grande do Sul, who are, according to *paulista* critics, rather exuberant conversationalists, speech-makers, and poets than hard workers. In spite of this *paulista* attitude, however, not only Brazil generally, but São Paulo particularly, owes much to Brazilians from the regions more famous for their delicious oranges, their fine cigars, and their poets, diplomats, and writers than for their factories, modern industries, and sky-scrapers. For some of the industrial leaders of São Paulo have been Brazilians from the North or from Rio Grande do Sul who found life too sleepy or too archaic in their native regions. The men from Ceará—an arid region—are particularly noted for their ability to migrate to populous cities or to pioneer areas of Brazil and become prosperous in some region characterized by one of two extremes: overpopulation or wilderness. A number of men from Ceará—men of Portuguese origin with Indian blood and perhaps the Indian nomadic tradition—have made good in São Paulo and Rio as industrial and commercial leaders and innovators; many have been the pioneers of Brazilian colonization in the vast Amazon region. They are, in more than one respect of ethos and activity, the modern *bandeirantes* of Brazil, successors of the old *paulistas*. If one accepts Mr. Waldo Frank's generalization, the *paulistas* are now bourgeois under "planless industrialism"; bourgeois "out from the workers, who are poor and spiritless and also directionless at the moment." Though this is somewhat exaggerated, there is some truth in it. The *cearenses*, or men from Ceará, also, fall into "planless industrialism" when they become bourgeois and prosperous in the big cities of Brazil. But most of them are going west. A number of them and of other Brazilians of the arid and semi-arid areas of Brazil—regions known for their cattle-raisers, rebels, wanderers, mystics, troubadours—are going west, or going to the Amazon, or are in the army and the navy. They are men eager for adventure. They are as warlike in spirit as the old *paulistas*, who, in contrast with the modern ones (whose presence in the army and the navy and in the risky pioneering colonization of the Amazon and the West is insignificant by comparison), fought in their day against the most belligerent Indians of the southern continent, against the Jesuits, and against the Spaniards.

The Brazilians from north-eastern Brazil—the arid, semi-arid, and coastal parts—are, like the original *paulistas*, typically *caboclo*, or indigenous, and more tellurically and traditionally Brazilian in spirit and behaviour than any other regional type. Most of them are—or, what has sometimes the same socio-psychological effect, imagine themselves to be—the descendants of some near or remote Indian brave; though sometimes this sort of "ethnocentrism"—to use Sumner's word—is contradicted by the almost Scandinavian blond hair and blue eyes of the self-styled *caboclo* or by the strong evidences of African blood in his not entirely Indian body.

As telluric and at the same time as traditional as the Brazilians of the North-east—Bahia included—are the old *paulistas* of São Paulo. One of them became the interpreter of his group when he expressed his pride in his ancestors' having been *paulistas* or Brazilians for more than four hundred years. But the old *paulistas* of São Paulo are becoming scarcer and scarcer, deeply affected as they have been in their anthropology and psychology by their increasing contact with growing numbers of Europeans and of Brazilians from other regions who have been attracted to São Paulo by its industrial prosperity. Almost as telluric and as traditional as the Brazilians of the north-eastern region are those of Rio de Janeiro, of Minas Geraes and of certain areas of Rio Grande do Sul, Pará, and other regions of Brazil.

There are still other aspects of Brazil, in point of regional diversity, that make the comparison with Spain relevant. For Spain is the classic—the most dramatic—example of a country where a stupid policy of centralization and of extreme unification has resulted in emphasizing the invincible power of regions and regional cultures. And, developing Senhor Ribeiro Conto's suggestion, Minas Geraes is in some ways the Castile of Brazil, and Ouro Preto its Toledo. Like the Castilian of Spain, the *mineiro* (inhabitant of Minas) is distinguished by his austerity and tendency to introspection, though far from having the intense mysticism and individualism of the real Castilian. Though apparently very simple, he is complex, subtle, and even sophisticated—as shown in the sense of humour that makes him smile at himself when necessary. This is not true of all *mineiros*. I have known *mineiros* with no sense of humour, who always take themselves seriously. But some of the deepest, driest, most sophisticated humour of Brazil comes from Minas Geraes. I never saw the *mineiro* poet Carlos Drumond de Andrade laugh; but he is a Brazilian master of dry humour, and as such he characteristically comes from Minas Geraes. The same thing is true of a typical *mineiro* whom I knew well when he was in Lisbon as a political *émigré* in 1930, after having been a very important man in Brazil. As *émigré*, he kept a magnificent sense of humour. He was the supreme realist of the entire group of *émigrés* with whom I came daily into contact, a group that included men who had occupied the most important positions as political leaders in Brazil. Some of them had fantastic ideas about what would happen in Brazil with the development of the Revolution of 1930, but that old *mineiro*, cigarette in mouth, had no illusions. He knew that a shrewd politician of a new type was to rule Brazil for many years, not only for a few months. He even outlined some of the contradictory but politically clever tendencies that the new regime would probably follow. Of himself and some of his political colleagues, he said: "We are politically dead." He was right in his psychological knowledge of Brazilians. He was prophetic without assuming the air of a prophet; he was too shy to do that, and had too much humour, too.

Because of a similar psychological knowledge of Brazilians displayed by Senhor Getulio Vargas, some observers have written that he is only by accident from Rio Grande do Sul: that in reality he is a *mineiro*. I think such observers are wrong. They appear not to know Rio Grande do Sul well. Senhor Vargas is the psychological, if not the logical, product of the obscure but very interesting area of the Rio Grande do Sul where he was born—the *missionera* area. It is true that there is a real antithesis between this area and the frame of mind one generally associates with the gaucho of the Rio Grande do Sul region. The men of the *mis-*

sionera area are not typical gauchos in behaviour, but, having more Indian blood than the typical gauchos and being the descendants of Indians educated and oppressed by Spanish Jesuits, they have in them something of their Jesuit masters: they are silent, introspective, subtle, realistic, distant, cold. They have also something of their brave ancestors, the "mission" Indians, whom the Jesuits were never able to dominate entirely. They are telluric, instinctive, fatalistic, proud, dramatic, almost tragic in their reactions to crises. Senhor Getulio Vargas seems to be a sort of Dr. Jekyll and Mr. Hyde in that he has in him something of the Jesuit but something also of the Indian. He is avid for power and domination, but he has also stood for the common people and for revolt against sterile conventions and powerful plutocratic groups. Characteristically he gave his first child the name of Luther; and the first thing he ever wrote as a young man was an article in defence of Zola. On the other hand, the Dr. Jekyll in Senhor Vargas has allowed religious and political persecution, and even Jesuitical despotism, to be practised in present-day Brazil by his assistants or under their indifferent eyes.

A few years ago I suggested that a psycho-sociological characterization of Brazilian regional types might be based on the various Brazilian ways of dancing their Carnival dances. Carnival is enthusiastically celebrated in Brazil, and the celebration lasts for three days. People dance in the clubs and theatres, and in the squares and streets. In some areas classes, races, sexes, and ages mingle as they do not do on ordinary days, with such a free democratic exuberance and a joy in fraternizing that one does not know how pagan it is, or how lyrically Christian: though largely pagan, it seems to have something Christian about it. But Carnival dances are only superficially the same in vast Brazil. In some areas they are "Dionysian," to use the old word revived by an American anthropologist to denote a well-known type of human behaviour; in other areas they are "Apollonian," or of an intermediate type. Based on the assumption that Carnival for the Brazilians is only an exaggeration—sometimes, I admit, a morbid exaggeration—of their ordinary and characteristic behaviour, I have suggested that through a careful study of the ways in which they dance their Carnival dances it is possible to classify their regional and sub-regional differences of temperament, ethos, and personality as well as to recognize their Brazilian unity of behaviour and their universality of human personality. The first results of such a study seem to indicate a considerable difference in the temperament or personality of such close neighbours as the gauchos and the *missioneros* of the Rio Grande do Sul region. Along with this study, I have suggested also a study of the characteristic Brazilian way of playing the very Anglo-Saxon game of association football, or soccer. The Brazilians play it as if it were a dance. This is probably the result of the influence of those Brazilians who have African blood, or who are predominantly African in their culture, for such Brazilians tend to reduce everything to dance —work and play alike—and this tendency is apparently becoming more and more general in Brazil and is not solely the characteristic of an ethnic or regional group. Since I published my first notes on these two subjects —the regional ways of dancing and of playing football, as a dance with something African to it—I have read Mr. Waldo Frank's brilliant comment that the tango is "a *sculptural* dance-music"; and elsewhere he tells us that, watching a group of men in Brazil playing soccer, he observed that they played "weaving the ball intricately (like the melodic line of a *samba*) to the goal."[8] It is almost the same remark that I had made in an article written in 1938, which I am sure Mr. Frank never saw, just as he never saw the one I published in 1940 about the Brazilian ways of dancing Carnival dances. I rejoice at the coincidence of his observation with mine, for I consider the author of *South American Journey* one of the few Americans who have written really illuminating pages on Brazil—illuminating for outsiders and for the Brazilians themselves. I know that sometimes he turns bombastic; but in his best pages he is enlightening and we should be thankful to him for them—and thankful also for his realization of Brazilian complexity and diversity, his respect for what regions and provinces mean in an intricate culture like that of Brazil. Too many foreign observers tend to see only what is metropolitan or picturesque, what is very progressive or very primitive or archaic: São Paulo or Rio, naked savages or the Amazon River. But it is between

8. Waldo Frank, *South American Journey* (New York, 1943), p. 50.

these two antagonistic extremes that the real Brazil lies, with its variety of regional situations.

Now, as under the Empire, there is a tendency to repress regional and provincial diversity to the advantage of political centralization and unity. On the other hand there are reformers who are against all centralization; they favour the total effacement of national as well as regional differences. In Brazil, regional energies seem to be too powerful to be easily repressed by mere political coercion or mere ideological wish. Senhor Vargas is too shrewd a politician to wish to be a new Philip II; and today there are fewer reformers impatient or intolerant of regional differences than some years ago. Some of them see that even the Soviet Union is returning to an intelligent policy of combining internationalism with regionalism.

The study of Brazilian social history and social conditions seems to show that there, as in other vast and complex nations, each man should be allowed to develop a particular loyalty to his basic community, region, or province. Though in his trans-national attachments he may go so far as to become a true citizen of the world, yet his status as member of a primary locality group seems essential to his personal and social health.

IV

ETHNIC AND SOCIAL CONDITIONS IN MODERN BRAZIL

As I showed in Chapter I, the European background of Brazilian history was itself only partially European. It was also African and Asiatic. It was complex. Portuguese ethnic and cultural complexity seems to have been, from the most remote beginning of Brazil, a stimulus to its differentiation from Europe and its independence from a strictly colonial or sub-European status.

Geographically Brazil is more closely related to Africa than to Europe. According to some plant and animal ecologists—one of them Professor Konrad Guenther—South America is in reality a continent distinct from North America. North America's climate and botanical and zoological characteristics remind one of Europe, while in the same respects South America's show a certain degree of independence and individuality. We must think of Brazil, Professor Guenther writes, referring to the marks of successive geological periods on the South American continent, as inhabited by a rich and diverse fauna, "which during all these long ages had time to develop in independence." [1] Such independence and di-

[1]. Konrad Guenther, *A Naturalist in Brazil: The Flora, the Fauna, and the People of Brazil*, trans. from the German by Bernard Miall (London, 1931), p. 160.

versity are interpreted by some authors as being perhaps the consequence of South America's having once been a number of islands, each evolving its own flora and fauna.

A different explanation is suggested by yet other geologists and ecologists: the age-long isolation of the continent and its division into many different topographical types. From the point of view of animal ecology, another ecologist—this one a Brazilian of German origin, Professor von Ihering—distinguishes six regions in Brazil: the Amazon region; the country to the south of Pará; the *Sertão* of the North-east; the interior of the southern States; the northern coastal zone, originally forest-clad; and the southern coastal zone, characterized by high grassy plains. These are only the regions; the sub-regions are many. As ecologists tell us, multiplicity of form is the essential characteristic of nature, especially of tropical nature, and if a European gardener tries to lay out a garden in Brazil he must follow "nature as a teacher," in the way suggested by Professor Guenther, and his garden must display the chief characteristic of the tropical vegetation, namely variety.

Tropical nature and the complexity of European background should have led the Portuguese pioneers who established themselves in Brazil as planters to practise variety in agricultural activity and production. But this did not happen, human behaviour never being logical. One-crop agriculture, especially sugar-cane, became the characteristic of the Brazilian natural and social landscape in the areas first dominated by Portuguese

Social Conditions 93

invasion. Later, sugar was to be replaced by coffee, but with the same unhealthy consequences for nature and for human society. In both spheres, essential harmony in the relations between living creatures was broken when one-crop agriculture, instead of diversification, was adopted. Tropical nature, being essentially many-sided, was perverted when only one particular plant was grown predominantly or exclusively over wide areas. And on the human side, as has been said, one type of social organization—a feudal or quasi-feudal one—was allowed to dominate.

Fortunately for Brazilians, tropical nature itself seems to have revolted against the uniformity imposed upon it by European one-crop agriculture. Small islands of secondary crops developed in the midst of the vast oceans of sugar-cane; tobacco, corn, and manioc were among the native and almost spontaneous forms of agriculture adopted from the Amerindians by the Portuguese, or cultivated only by nomadic Amerindians. And somewhat the same thing happened in the sphere of human ecology: the Indians, for instance, revolted against the imposition upon them of the plantation-slave status. Some became collaborators only with frontiers-men, and most of them developed into fierce enemies of the one-crop planter who wanted them as his slaves. But the Brazilian Indians were nomadic in habit and taste. Sedentary life, agricultural routine, the monotony of labour on the plantations meant death for them. This explains why Negroes from Africa were imported in such large numbers to Portuguese America and why their descendants are today such an important element in the ethnic composition and social structure of Brazil.

If the equilibrium of Brazilian nature was dramatically disturbed when sugar-cane was made the single basis of Portuguese domination, the introduction of the African Negro in the sugar regions is regarded by some historians and sociologists as an even greater disturbance —the Negro being introduced into areas to which he did not rightly belong. It may not, however, have constituted so serious an ecological disturbance as these authors believe. Henry Bates, a British scientist who spent a number of years in Brazil during the middle of the nineteenth century, came to the conclusion that the Negro was happier in tropical America than the Indian was. Bates contrasted the Indian's "constitutional dislike to the heat" with the Negro's perfect adaptation to it. His reasoned judgment was that the Negro, not the Indian, is "the true child of tropical climes";[2] the true child of tropical Brazil as well as of tropical Africa.

From the standpoint of man's relationship to nature, the Negro's adaptation to the climate and other physical conditions of Brazil seems to have been perfect. From the social standpoint he was culturally better prepared than the nomadic Amerindian to adjust himself to the status of slave—plantation and domestic slave—in Portuguese America. His adaptation to American condi-

[2] *The Naturalist on the River Amazon, Humboldt Library of Science* (New York, [n. d.], I, 725.

tions was as happy as that of the sugar-cane plant, his symbiotic companion in the task of modifying the Brazilian landscape from an area of virgin forest to one dominated by plantation colonization and one-crop agriculture.

Some of the millions of Negroes imported to Brazilian plantations were obtained from areas of the most advanced Negro culture. This explains why there were African slaves in Brazil—men of Mohammedan faith and intellectual training—who were culturally superior to some of their European, white, Catholic masters. More than one foreigner who visited Brazil in the nineteenth century was surprised to find that the leading French bookseller of the Empire's capital had among his customers Mohammedan Negroes of Bahia; through him these remarkable Negroes, some of them ostensibly Christian but actually Mohammedan, imported expensive copies of their sacred books for secret study. Some of them maintained schools, and the Mohammedan Negroes in Bahia had mutual-aid societies, through which a number of slaves were liberated.

In the province of Minas Geraes, too, the slaves had mutual-aid societies. And the American Ewbank, while in Brazil (1845–46), once dined with a Bahian planter who told him that the slaves of Salvador (capital city of Bahia and formerly the capital of colonial Brazil) preserved their own language, organized clubs, and nurtured revolutionary schemes that their Pernambuco brethren repeatedly attempted to carry out; some Bahian slaves were able to "write Arabic fluently" and were "vastly superior to their masters."[3] I have been fortunate in finding evidence confirming what Ewbank was told and proving that, besides the merely strong slaves good only for field work, many culturally advanced Negroes were brought to Brazil. Perhaps no other American colony had, among its Africans imported for labour, so large a number of the latter type. And this importation of culturally advanced and aesthetically attractive Negroes from the African areas most influenced by Mohammedan civilizing power explains why in Brazil, probably more commonly than in any other American colony, beautiful Negresses become the famous mistresses of wealthy and prominent Portuguese merchants in Bahia and Ouro Preto, Rio and Recife. Some of them surpassed their white or Amerindian rivals in prestige. In Minas Geraes more than one became rich and married their daughters to socially important young men, European or Brazilian white. One such was Jacintha de Siqueira, whom I found named in an interesting genealogical document in some family archives of that region; many a Brazilian now prominent in political or professional life has her blood in his veins.

Negroes are now rapidly disappearing in Brazil, merging into the white stock; in some areas the tendency seems to be towards the stabilization of mixed-bloods in a new ethnic type, similar to the Polynesian. Though

3. Thomas Ewbank, *Life in Brazil, or The Land of the Cocoa and the Palm* (London, 1856), p. 441.

this tendency is usually found among peasants and immigrants, there have been other Jacinthas in the history of aristocratic Brazilian families; they are rare, but they have existed, and they are the subject of gossip. Ewbank wrote, in the book already quoted on Brazil at the beginning of the reign of Pedro II: "I have passed black ladies in silks and jewelry, with male slaves in livery behind them. Today one rode past in her carriage, accompanied by a liveried footman and a coachman. Several have white husbands. The first doctor of the city is a colored man; so is the President of the Province." And he describes the Viscountess of C—— as "tinged." [4]

There has been, and still is, social distance between different groups of the population. But social distance is—more truly today than in the colonial age or during the Empire (when slavery was central in the social structure)—the result of class consciousness, rather than of race or colour prejudice. Since the Brazilian attitude is one of large tolerance towards people who have African blood but who can pass for white, nothing is more expressive than the popular saying: "Anyone who escapes being an evident Negro is white." Sir Richard Burton observed in Imperial Brazil that "here, all men, especially free men, who are not black, are white; and often a man is officially white, but naturally almost a Negro. This is directly opposed to the system in the United States where all men who are not unmixed white are black." [5] Visiting Brazil half a century after Burton,

4. *Ibid.*, p. 266.
5. *The Highlands of Brazil* (London, 1867), I, p. 393.

Bryce included it among the countries where the distinction between the races is a distinction "of rank or class rather than of colors." [6]

Even during colonial days, if a person was politically or socially important the fact that his or her ethnic past had some direct contact with Africa was robbed of significance by present position: he or she passed for white. I have examined this Brazilian process of sociological "Aryanization" in more than one book, in which the Brazilian solution of the problems arising from race contact is contrasted with other solutions and is explained in the light of the peculiar social and cultural experience of the Portuguese as a transition people between Europe and Africa.

Another transition people between Europe and Africa, the Russian, is now revealing to the world a new and in some ways successful type of social organization that includes miscegenation (especially Euro-Asiatic race mixture) among its solutions of social problems. In more than one aspect of its ethnic and social situation, Brazil reminds one of Russia; it is almost an American Russia.[7] The experiment in ethnic and cultural bi-continentalism begun in Portugal centuries ago took a new dimension in Brazil: three races and cultures are fused under conditions that, broadly speaking,

---

6. James Bryce, *Sou'' America, Observations and Impressions* (New York, 1913), p. 470.
7. The author's comparison of Brazil to Russia was made prior to the same comparison by Count Keyserling. It is here repeated from the author's essay, "*Aspectos de um seculo de transição*," published in *Livro do Nordeste* (Recife, 1925).

are socially democratic, though as yet productive of only a very imperfect social democracy, defective both in its economic basis and in its political forms of expression. All imperfections admitted, however, Brazil stands today as a community from whose experiment in miscegenation other communities may profit. Probably in no other complex modern community are problems of race relations being solved in a more democratic or Christian way than in Portuguese America. And Brazil's experiment does not indicate that miscegenation leads to degeneration.

Professor Charles R. Stockard's conclusions—that "mongrelization among widely different human stocks has very probably caused the degradation and even the elimination of certain groups"; that "the extinction of several ancient stocks has apparently followed very closely the extensive absorption of alien slaves"; and that "if one considers the histories of some of the South European and Asia Minor countries from a strictly biological and genetic point of view, a very definite correlation between the amalgamation of the whites and the negroid slaves and the loss of intellectual and social power will be found" [8]—do not obtain their best support in the Luso-Brazilian experience. It is true that Portugal has not today the intellectual and social power that it had four centuries ago; but this is also true of "Aryan" Holland and "Aryan" Denmark. According to Professor Stockard's theory, Brazil, where miscege-

---

8. *The Genetic and Endocrine Basis for Differences in Form and Behavior* (Philadelphia, 1941), pp. 37–38.

nation proceeded more freely than in Portugal or Spain, should be vastly inferior in intellectual and social power, not only to Portugal, but to quasi-white South American nations like Argentina and Chile. Objective studies of Latin American national or regional variety in achievement and cultural development do not seem to confirm the inferiority of mestizo Brazil to its more "Aryan" neighbours. It is in Brazil and not in the more "Aryan" countries of Latin America that one finds today the most vigorously creative group of young architects, young painters, and young composers of Latin America and perhaps of the entire American continent; and, in mestizo Brazil, the most creative group of medical scientists engaged in the study of the so-called tropical diseases and of problems peculiar to tropical areas. Brazil is universally known for the work of scientists like Cruz, Chagas, Fontes, Roquette Pinto, Almeida, Silva Mello, Vital Brazil, and Lins. The successful experiments of Brazilian investigators (some of them mestizo) with anti-venom serums to nullify the effects of poisonous snakes save many lives in many countries every year.

Another fact that seems to refute those who emphatically generalize on the social and intellectual effects of what they call "mongrelization" is that for years the Brazilian areas producing the largest number of political leaders and men of literary, scientific, and artistic talent have been the areas notable for the extension and intensity of ethnic amalgamation and cultural interpenetration: the North-east (including Bahia

SOCIAL CONDITIONS 101

and Sergipe), Rio de Janeiro, Minas Geraes, and São Paulo. During the Empire, Bahia was known as the "Brazilian Virginia" because most of the cabinet presidents came from that province. Some of the cabinet presidents of the Brazilian Empire, though their formal behaviour was like that of members of the British Parliament, were men with Negro blood. And though the qualities of the Brazilian statesmen during the Empire period were imitative rather than creative, some of them were remarkable for their political talent as well as for their tact and ability as diplomats.

As an empire, Brazil was a country whose stability and peace contrasted with the turbulent political life of most of the Latin American republics. Even then it was ruled by an aristocracy democratic enough to allow men with Negro blood to become its members, though it remained largely white or quasi white in its composition. The Republican period, however, has seen the increasing rise to political power and to intellectual, industrial, and ecclesiastical leadership of Brazilians of African origin. As a political system the Republic established in Brazil in 1889 remained, as the Empire had been, more imitative than creative. Honesty among public men decreased; there was also a decrease in the elegance and dignity that had become characteristic of the Brazilian Parliament in the days of Dom Pedro II. On the other hand, there was an increase in efficiency in practical matters: some of the new political leaders were notable for their ability to deal with economic and sanitary problems, which had been somewhat neglected by the Empire. And a few surrounded themselves with scientists and engineers who began to do really creative work.

It was not until the establishment of the Republic that a series of courageous projects for harbours and wharves, water-works, sanitation schemes, city paving, draining, and beautifying began to develop in Brazil, along with plans for a more efficient commercial organization of coffee production. Brazil fell in love with material progress. And in most of these plans one can detect the dynamic impatience of the Brazilians who entered public life with the 1889 Republic: their eagerness to make their country modern, progressive, different from Portugal, different from its colonial or monarchical structure.

Of the new Republican leaders a considerable number were mixed-bloods, men of modest rather than of aristocratic origin. They seem to have made of the Republican regime an expression of their own eagerness for a new and better social status. This may explain the political importance assumed by the army in the new regime. In contrast with the navy, which took special pride in having as officers only Caucasian whites or Indo-Caucasians and sons of aristocratic or wealthy bourgeois families; and in contrast also with the clergy, which during the Empire was chiefly white and aristocratic or bourgeois—the Brazilian army started developing into a socially and ethnically democratic organization, with a number of officers of very modest social origin and some with considerable Indian and Negro blood in their veins. These men assumed an active and dynamic part in the nation's political life. When the Brazilian plantation system began to disintegrate—a disintegration that proceeded rapidly after the abolition of slavery (one year before the founding of the Republic in 1889)—the army and the Church remained the only two organized groups in the country. And of the two the army was the more liberal, progressive, and democratic; the Church, the more conservative, though seldom illiberal or violently opposed to social reform.

Not a few of the younger army officers had come under the influence of the Positivism of Comte, and the most enthusiastic of them were convinced that here they had not *a* solution, but *the* solution, of all Brazilian problems. Another group of Republican idealists—a civilian one—were just as convinced, on the basis of what political, juridical, and financial knowledge they had gained from their reading of Anglo-American authors, that a federal and democratic constitution copied from that of the United States would solve all Brazilian troubles.

Between these two groups of extreme ideologues there were Republican leaders whose method was the British one of dealing with each problem as it presented itself, rather than according to any rigid philosophical system or logical ideology. Among this third group of new and realistic leaders there were, as in the two others, Negroid Brazilians remarkable for their eagerness to rise to power as well as for their intellectual ability and personal charm—men like Francisco Glicerio and Nilo Peçanha; just as there were descendants of European non-Portuguese immigrants who had arrived in Brazil as peasants or artisans—men like Lauro Müller, son of a German, and Paulo Frontin, son of a Frenchman. Psychologically and sociologically they were in the same boat: eager to rise socially through a successful political career as leaders of the new regime in Brazil. And the shrewdest seem to have thought that the most intelligent thing to do was not to commit themselves to a definite philosophical system or political ideology, whose prestige might rapidly disappear, but to give themselves to a cause that would remain for a long time dear to almost all Brazilians: the cause of material progress. Hence the plans for general improvement as the most characteristic expression of Republican activity in Brazil.

It was at this point that Brazil went into debt on a great scale, borrowing from European bankers the necessary gold for building harbours, wharves, waterworks, sanitation plants, avenues, railroads, battle-ships, and what not. Though much of this money was spent extravagantly, no one can deny that the leaders of "the First Republic" gave Brazil public works and sanitary public conveniences that were essential to social, and not only economic, development.

Such material works and accomplishments should not be under-estimated. They were valuable; they were the first great contribution of the Republican system of government to Brazilian progress. For now the members of the land- and slave-holding aristocracy were being replaced as Brazil's political leaders by a new element of the population, an element considerably different from its predecessors in social origin, ethnic composition, and economic and intellectual interests. Most of those predecessors had taken the patriarchal, feudal, or aristocratic view of Brazilian social problems; they had regarded sugar (and, to a certain extent, coffee) as the great Brazilian problem; they had considered themselves the heads of large families of sugar- or coffee-producing slaves or semi-slaves—large families whose constellation was Brazil. The new leaders, some of them remote or second- or third-generation descendants of slaves or of peasants or modest immigrants from Europe, had a more democratic experience and outlook on life, though not enough to become effective leaders in the social reconstruction of Brazil. Most of them were too eager for a rise in social status to trouble over any other social or human problem, with the exception of sanitary improvements in large towns—a narrowly bourgeois facet of the whole group of social problems confronting the Brazilian people. In regard to economic problems they remained conservative.

Out of the contact of some of the new Republican leaders with the dwindling power of a rapidly disintegrating sugar and coffee aristocracy, there arose a plan for the defence of Brazilian coffee production—a plan that stands as one of the most original contributions of Portuguese America (increasingly mestizo and even Negroid in the composition of its political and intellectual elite) to the science of economics and to the then very vague technique of government control of markets. According to an American specialist in the subject, the Brazilian "valorization" plan for coffee control in 1905 has been followed by Ecuador in regard to cacao, by Mexico for control of its henequen, by British Malaya and Ceylon for rubber, by Cuba for sugar, by Egypt for cotton, and by Italy for citrate of lime. In addition, as the same writer points out, valorization has been applied to numerous commodities in a purely domestic market, a familiar example being the efforts of the Federal Farm Board to raise the price of wheat in the United States. The term *valorization*, we are told by Mr. Charles R. Whittlesey in his article on this subject in the *Encyclopedia of the Social Sciences*, "was introduced into English-speaking countries about 1906 from Brazil where it [*valorização*] had been applied to measures regulating the marketing of coffee."[9]

Successful in the valorization of their coffee, the first Republican leaders of Brazil neglected human problems —developed no plan for the "valorization" of the common people. Keen though they were in regard to financial matters and problems of material progress, they failed in dealing with human problems because they did not get close to human, social, and cultural reality; for example, they neglected the very important problem of directing the transition of a large number of Brazilians from slave work to free work. Apparently the most realistic of them considered that such problems were

9. "Valorization," *Encyclopedia of the Social Sciences*, XV, 211–212.

not for statesmen but for humanitarians, missionaries, lyric poets. Moreover, a few of them—men with slave Negro blood—did not want to appear as champions of a cause whose defence would emphasize an hereditary personal element that they were eager to forget and to have others forget; hence they concentrated on material progress—on borrowing and building, on attracting foreign capital and foreign labour. This latter—the attracting of foreign capital and labour—was typical of the narrowly economic policy pursued for the material Europeanization of Brazil, especially in the coast towns. Little attention was paid to the human, the broadly social and cultural, side of the problem of European colonization.

Early in the nineteenth century the deliberate importation of European immigrants began, to be increased a few years later, when the British took measures against the slave trade so severe that only a few contraband shiploads of Negroes were successfully brought to Brazilian plantations. Statesmen of the last years of the Empire realized that because of the scarcity of slave labour the prospects for Brazilian agriculture were far from brilliant. But the problem that had to be faced was not merely economic: it was social as well. How could a country dominated by the plantation system, one-crop agriculture, and a feudal organization, attract Europeans eager to find in America freer and more comfortable conditions than in their native countries? How could a country almost morbidly devoted to coffee-planting and to sugar-cane-planting, on immense estates held by a small number of landlords, be changed into a country of peasant coffee-planting and diversified agriculture without going through a violent revolution? A great planter of the last years of the Empire, Moreira de Barros, when he held the portfolio of Foreign Affairs, very realistically pointed out that European immigrants to Brazil would "only work for their own hand and on their own lands." What the planters wanted, in the way of immigrants, was a type content to be merely the passive successors of the plantation slaves—and this the European immigrants were not willing to become.

How generally the human aspect of the problem was neglected in favour of the economic is shown by the attempt of Empire statesmen to bring Chinese coolies to the plantations to take the place of the Negro slaves. This new form of slavery would have been introduced into Portuguese America if in 1883, when the project was so seriously considered that a Mr. Tong King Sing came to Brazil to discuss it, public feeling in Rio and other cities had not risen against the great planters, whose narrow feudalistic habits and economic interests made them blind to broad national problems. This year of 1883 is an historic milestone in the struggle for the economic democratization of Brazil, because it was then that the coffee-planting interests lost an important battle to preserve a system that—though originally creative for Brazilian agriculture and society—had, with the developing of new needs and conditions, become wholly parasitic and unhealthy.

The fact that public opinion was so strong against

the introduction of Chinese coolies shows that, at least since the last years of the Empire, there has been a public opinion in Brazil. Superficial interpreters of Brazilian life who maintain that the only government for Brazil is a paternalistic dictatorship, because "there is no public opinion in the country," forget such episodes as the vigorous popular reaction of 1883. A good and liberal man was then emperor, but he probably would have acted as the great coffee and sugar planters wanted him to act—in favour of their private and feudalistic interests—if public opinion had not manifested itself so emphatically.

For at that time the Brazilians had the right to express their feelings at public meetings and in the press. Indeed, so free was the press that Abolitionists and Republicans sometimes referred to Dom Pedro II as "Pedro Banana," meaning that though an emperor he was too much the weak instrument of powerful private interests—more like a soft banana than like a man. Brazil has had other rulers of the paternalistic type who have been given similar nicknames because, though good, honest, well-meaning men, they have considered powerful private interests above popular interests and national needs: "Tio Pita," or Uncle Pita, for instance—President Pessoa being so called by his political opponents because of his alleged tendencies towards what might be termed avuncular benevolence. Paternalistic government seems not to work well when social conditions cease to favour paternalism and begin to demand strong leadership as directly responsible as possible to the people or to its most vigorous and best-educated elements. It appears to be actually harmful when it does not act as a transition regime, interested in incorporating the common people into the civic life of the nation.

But popular reaction was not the only force that served to frustrate the project of importing coolies. Another force appeared, whose motive was not so much humanitarianism, probably, as it was the hope to compete with coffee- and sugar-producing Brazil. I mean the British Empire. A significant letter on the subject was published (December 1883) in *The Anti-Slavery Reporter* of London—a letter signed by Charles H. Allen and addressed to the Right Hon. the Earl Granville, K.G., etc., Her Majesty's Principal Secretary of State for Foreign Affairs. The writer reported that British abolitionists had made plain to Mr. Tong King Sing the extreme danger that Chinese coolies imported into Brazil, under contract, would virtually become slaves; and he ended: "I am desired by the Committee to thank your lordship for the prompt measures taken by your lordship's directions, to call the attention of Her Majesty's Representatives at Rio and Pekin to the question of Chinese immigration into Brazil, and to express a hope that your lordship will request those Ministers still to keep this subject before them, as future similar schemes may, at any moment, be introduced in which the planters might have to deal with gentlemen less astute and not so large-hearted as Mr. Tong King Sing."

More than once, great powers that have outlived slavery or semi-slavery have befriended liberal, democratic reforms in weaker and less-advanced countries; for such countries, in continuing to keep slaves or serfs, may become dangerous competitors of the great powers in agricultural production. This may explain why the Brazilian liberals have at various times had the support even of European politicians notable for realism rather than for humanitarianism in their foreign policy. It may also explain the obverse: why even dictatorial governments in Brazil and other Latin American countries have sometimes had the support of liberal and democratic leaders of great powers interested not so much in democratization as in the rise of the acquisitive capacity of weaker nations.

As soon as the coffee-planters of Brazil suspected that the slave business was doomed, the most enterprising among them sought to attract European peasants to the coffee estates through the system known as *parceria*, a system not far removed from serfdom. It is true, as objective critics of the *parceria* system have pointed out, that the colonist had the satisfaction of considering himself an independent worker; but, as he started with a large debt, never owned land, and earned no wages, his lot was a poor one if crops failed or the *fazendeiro* proved to be unfair. The colonist arrived "owing for the passage of himself and family, and was given a house and a quantity of food of the country; he cultivated a certain number of coffee trees, or allotment of sugar cane, took the harvest to the owner's mill and received half the result after milling."[10] Under this system he

10. Elliott, *op. cit.*, p. 61.

was entirely dependent upon the planter's fair play; and, as emphasized by some apologists for the *parceria* system, the hard-working Bavarians and Holsteiners in São Paulo often paid off their debts in four years and then had money in hand—a fact that speaks well for the fairness of some coffee-planters in their dealings with the European peasant, since they might have kept him indefinitely as a semi-slave, always indebted and always dependent. It may be added that it was not Germans, but North Italians, who proved to be the best successors to Negro slaves on the coffee plantations.

Though there was considerable friction between planters and European colonists during the transition phase from slavery to free labour, an adjustment was eventually reached when a government agency known as *Patronato Agricola* instituted a moderate control over the relations between *fazendeiros* and their new white workers, to whom at least medical care had now to be given. Although Italian colonization in São Paulo was so successful that about one-third of its present population are of Italian blood and are prominent in business and in society, this was the only State in which the new adjustment was really a success. For the areas where European colonization has markedly succeeded are those that were most nearly free from any inheritance of the plantation system: Rio Grande do Sul, Santa Catharina, Paraná, parts of Minas Geraes, Rio de Janeiro, and Espirito Santo. All attempts to establish European colonists in the neighbourhood of the old plantation areas—Bahia, Rio de Janeiro, Pernambuco—were failures.

On the other hand, failure was also the lot of most of the Anglo-American colonists who went to nineteenth-century Brazil because it was a slavery country and they were used to being owners of Negroes and their superiors. Dozens of disappointed Southerners went to Brazil after the South was defeated in the Civil War, and very few were successful or happy in their new home. It seems that most of them went there with very little money and so could not establish themselves as planters and slave-owners and live the life they had been accustomed to in the Old South. To start life as independent farmers in pioneering areas of Brazil—as European peasants did successfully in southern Brazil—was no easy task for men who had grown up having Negroes do all their heavy work for them. Some tried to grow cotton, but under very adverse conditions. These conditions and other factors probably explain the many failures.

Almost thirty years ago an American geographer, Mr. L. E. Elliott, inquiring what had become of those fellow countrymen of his who had gone to Brazil after the Civil War, was told a story that he describes as "comedy instead of tragedy." It is told of the group that settled in Santa Barbara to grow watermelons. One year, just as the crop ripened (so the story goes), cholera broke out in São Paulo; the sale of melons was forbidden and the growers faced ruin. As a new United

States consul had just been appointed to Santos by the new President of the United States—Cleveland, a Democrat—the Southerners decided that the new consul must also be a good Democrat. On his arrival, therefore, they wrote him a letter of congratulation and told him of their difficult economic situation. The consul, it seems, replied cordially, suggesting that, as consul, he should visit them; and received posthaste a warm welcome from the Southerners. "The afternoon of his arrival at the colony found the entire population drawn up on the platform, a southern Colonel at the head of the deputation. The train rolls up, a first-class compartment door opens, a gentleman steps out with a suitcase, and walks up to the Colonel with outstretched hand. It was the consul, but a consul as black as the ace of spades. It is said that the Colonel, rising nobly to the occasion . . . shook the hand of the consul, and that he and the other Southerners gave the official the time of his life; but when he departed they vowed that never, never again would they trust a Democratic administration." [11]

Most of the descendants of the Civil War Southerners in Brazil have learned to forget their prejudice against Negroes and mestizos. Some have had to come into contact with Brazilian senators or prominent business leaders or professional men not purely white: mixed-blood white and Negro, not only white and Amerindian, though the commonest mixture in São Paulo has been the white-Amerindian. This is the dominant mixture at the base of the proud old aristocracy

11. Elliott, *op. cit.*, pp. 65–66.

Social Conditions

of that State, as well as of other regions of Brazil where it is still a matter of pride for an old family to have among its ancestors an Indian, generally idealized as a hero of the wars against the French or the Dutch (who in the sixteenth and seventeenth centuries tried to conquer parts of Brazil), admired as a fighter against the Portuguese, or honoured as a princess—the beautiful daughter of some powerful Indian chief. The first cardinal of Latin America, Cardinal Arcoverde, was the descendant of a Pernambuco Indian princess of the sixteenth century: a Brazilian Pocahontas. He was proud of his Amerindian blood. He was also insistent on the need, for Brazil, of a native clergy; that is, consisting of men born in Brazil or integrated in Brazilian life, instead of one made up entirely of foreign priests and monks. He was not narrowly nationalistic, but he probably saw the danger for Latin American countries of being kept as intellectual and economic colonies of Europe with the indirect assistance of priests who, being European, would usually have a European attitude of autocratic paternalism (if not of absolute superiority) towards Amerindian or Indo-Hispanic or Afro-Hispanic populations.

Such was the extent of Indianism in Brazil, not only in literature but in daily life, that, when Brazil separated from Portugal and there was widespread feeling against any Portuguese attempt at re-conquest, a considerable number of distinguished Brazilian families had their family names changed to Amerindian names. Most of these were poetic—names of rivers or plants; but some were very prosaic, though expressive—names of fish associated with market and kitchen, like Carapeba.

The Indians of Brazil were remarkable, as modern scientists have pointed out, for their knowledge of the flora and fauna of the country; and to the present day many rivers, plants, animals, mountains, towns, and drugs have, in Brazil, not Portuguese but Amerindian names. According to a European scientist—the Professor Konrad Guenther already quoted—in Brazil as in Spanish America not only do many families point with pride to Indian chieftains in their past (a fact that I have already pointed out), but among the descendants of Indians in some regions the Brazilian seems indeed to be reverting to the Indian type; while the Africans are apparently being gradually and peacefully absorbed by the white-Indian population, no fresh recruits from Africa having come in for years.[12] This German ecologist of pre-Nazi days was sympathetic to race-mixture and Indianism as a means by which the Brazilians could create a home-grown civilization, evolved organically from its environment, with its various departments of activity united at their source: Nature. In this connection he found that the many Indian names of natural objects form a connecting link with the Indian source of Brazilian culture, and recommended that more should be done along the same line through popularizing Indian animal stories among Brazilian children of today. Novels like those of José de Alencar—the Brazilian Cooper—and the larger utilization of Indian motives

12. Guenther, *op. cit.*, pp. 371–372.

Social Conditions

in Brazilian modern art might increase the Brazilian pride in their Amerindian origins and in the natural foundations of their culture.

One should not forget that the Indians of Brazil were a forest people with a forest culture. The remaining Indians and the survivals of indigenous cultures are a very important element to be reckoned with in any cultural policy directed towards a deeper harmony between Brazilians and their natural environment. Such a policy of harmony finds a strong basis in the attitude of the Portuguese colonists in regard to intermarriage with the Amerindian population: an attitude of tolerance and sometimes enthusiasm for Amerindian physical and cultural differences.

The very fact that the Amerindians, nomadic as they were, made bad slaves for the first sugar-cane plantations and fought with remarkable vigour against the Portuguese who tried to enslave them created a legend of their "independence," "bravery," and "nobility." This legend is responsible even today for the Brazilian tendency to consider the Amerindian superior to the Negro, though a strictly scientific study of Amerind contributions to the cultural development of Brazil would probably lead one to a different conclusion. However, the enthusiasm of most Brazilians for the Jesuit missionaries of the sixteenth century and the early part of the seventeenth century—priests who did their best to respect the freedom of the Amerindians proclaimed by the Pope and the King of Portugal—is based on the same legend.

The work of the Jesuits has been continued in recent years by an officer of the Brazilian army whose activity as head of the Brazilian Federal Department for the Protection of the Indians has surpassed that of any missionary. I refer to General Candido Mariano da Silva Rondon, himself a descendant of Indians. Rondon began his work as a lieutenant, in 1890, when a government expedition under Major Gomes Carneiro went to the Bororos region in central Brazil to establish telegraphic contact between that part of the then young Republic and the more civilized regions. At that time an intelligent policy of friendly relations with Indian tribes was started by the Brazilian army. This policy has followed the plan for assimilating the Indians sketched at the beginning of the nineteenth century by José Bonifacio, leader of the Independence movement in Brazil and the greatest statesman that Portuguese America has had. Bonifacio, a scientist with a European reputation, has been described as, essentially, a practical idealist. As has been pointed out by the students of his life and ideas, he had as his main concern the development of Brazil into a characteristically American nation, free from European race prejudices. A basic idea in his program of social organization was the assimilation of the Indian as well as of the Negro. Nor did he fear the mestizo or the mixed-blood. On the contrary, he opposed the segregation policy pursued by the Jesuits in some parts of Brazil. He had little interest in any vague and fictitious equality of Amerindians before the

SOCIAL CONDITIONS 119

law, but advocated their assimilation by a Brazilian culture that would be enriched by them.

Brazil still has to face the problem of assimilating certain Amerindian tribes as well as those groups of Negroes whose culture remains largely African. Although there are Brazilians with European prejudices who regard as disgraceful any departure from European and Roman Catholic standards of morals, law, and custom, the general tendency among broad-minded Brazilians is to maintain, towards such Africans as well as towards Indians, a policy of slow and intelligent assimilation, in which the assimilating group may incorporate into its culture certain values of general interest or artistic importance selected from characteristics preserved by deeply differentiated sub-groups or sub-cultures. A similar policy will probably be followed in regard to the Germans and other European colonists, and also to the Japanese in the areas of southern Brazil where they have lived segregated for more than a generation. Some students think that Portuguese Brazilian cultural values, regarded as basic to the development of Brazil as a nation and a broadly Christian community (including the Portuguese language and Portuguese freedom from race prejudice), should be emphasized as general values. There should be no subordination, however, of non-Portuguese sub-groups or sub-cultures to a rigidly uniform Luso-Brazilian or Portuguese-Brazilian culture or "race." With a broad democratic policy like this—an ethnically and socially democratic policy—Brazil would become an ideal country for Europeans tired of narrow race and class prejudices and of illiberal nationalism and religious sectarianism. Not only peasants and artisans would have favourable conditions for expressing their creative power, but also the proficient agriculturist, the expert fruit-grower, and the stock-raiser. For, as the American geographer Elliott perceived, the hardy and determined pioneer still has a chance in Brazil—though it will not be possible for him to be the individualist that he was a century or a half-century ago, when there was no efficient public service for protecting the Amerindians or for conserving the forests and the mineral resources. Such human and natural values are now protected by laws inspired by a real concern for the interests of the Brazilian community rather than by a wish to favour individual exploitation. The program of the present Council of Immigration and Colonization of Brazil (which has for leader an army officer as public-spirited as Rondon—Colonel Lima Camara) includes "controlled colonization" and mixed "colonization nuclei" for both Brazilians (thirty per cent) and aliens (seventy per cent). This is an old idea of Bonifacio's.

Brazil is famous for its "white," or peaceful, revolutions. Its independence was the result of one of these. Though it remained an empire when all the other Latin American countries were republics, a peaceful revolution transformed it into a republic. A peaceful revolution transformed it from a slave-holding country into one where everybody is born free. A peaceful revolution separated Church from State, solving a problem that has been the source of much friction in other Latin countries. An almost peaceful revolution—that of 1930—has favoured Brazilian town labourers with a social legislation that is, in theory if not always in practice, one of the most advanced of our day. Brazil will therefore probably be able to revolutionize immigration policies without violence either to immigrants or to old residents. Much remains to be done in connection with the colonization of unoccupied land by Brazilians and by immigrants. The "valorization" of the Brazilian native peasant is urgently needed.

Ill-health, especially that caused by malaria, ankylostomiasis, tuberculosis, syphilis, and the Masson-Pirajá disease, seems to be responsible for the laziness of which the Brazilian *caboclo,* or native peasant, has been accused by superficial foreign critics. In everything Brazilian that is unpleasant to their eyes, these critics see evidence of the ill effects of race mixture or tropical climate. More than fifty years ago a Brazilian author who held some of Bonifacio's ideas, Sylvio Romero, wrote that the mixed-bloods formed the mass of the Brazilian population, making the point that both Amerindian and Negro were "inarticulate" in Brazilian society and culture. It was then the fashion for sophisticated Brazilians to cover up everything of Negro origin that they could: blood, food, customs, words, and every other influence or element that could be concealed. A characteristic of the country today is that this almost Freudian censorship of mestizo spontaneity is no longer a strong force in Brazilian psychology or cultural and social life; and the consequence of this sort of psychoanalytic cure for what was a national complex is that Brazilian music, cookery, literature, and art are more and more expressing popular life, needs, and values.

As a whole, the Brazilians have what psychiatrists call a traumatic past. Slavery was their great trauma. For many, colour remained for some time the disagreeable reminder of an unhappy social situation or an injurious episode in their past. Certain officers of the traditionally democratic Brazilian army have sought to impede its development into an ethnically and socially democratic institution by trying to introduce into it racial restrictions by which Negroes and obviously Negroid men could not become officers; and this may be considered a neurotic expression of that complex. But it is an almost isolated one. The general tendency in present-day Brazil is to regard slavery as an episode over and done with, having only a social bearing on the history of the total Brazilian personality. Even Brazilians with a family or individual past that has nothing to do with Africa, biologically or ethnically, join Negroid Brazilians in a feeling, now general though not universal, that nothing is honestly or sincerely Brazilian that denies or hides the influence of the Amerindian and the Negro.

V

BRAZILIAN FOREIGN POLICY AS CONDITIONED BY BRAZIL'S ETHNIC, CULTURAL, AND GEOGRAPHICAL SITUATION

BRAZIL's national status is not an expression of race consciousness, for no single pure or nearly pure race made the country. No European people engaged in colonizing America was less animated by a race-superiority or race-purity complex than the Portuguese, an almost non-European nation. Its unity or purity *mystique* was one of religion or religious status—the Roman Catholic religion or the Christian status—and not one of race.

Brazil's national status is an ethnically negative one. Few modern nations are so heterogeneous from an ethnic point of view as the only Portuguese-speaking republic of the American continent. In Brazil no ethnic minority or majority really exercises an absolute, systematic, and permanent cultural and social domination over politically or economically less active elements of the population. Among a few whites there may be a desire to dominate the many coloured members of the Brazilian community, but these few are too inarticulate as an ethnic or cultural aristocracy to be seriously considered a decided imperial influence on domestic cultural policy or a significant factor in determining, in whatever way a culture or race-superiority complex might affect it, the foreign policy of Brazil.

As a national community Brazil, it seems to me, has to be interpreted as a community increasingly conscious of its status or destiny as a social and ethnic democracy and aware of its pioneering in this field. As such, it is second only to the Soviet Union as a community quasi officially, if not officially, committed to a frankly equalitarian racial policy. Even Mexico seems to be less tolerant of Negroes than Brazil is. From my drawing such comparisons, however, no one should understand me as implying that Brazil is a perfect ethnic democracy. It is not.

Brazil has become prominent as a community inclined towards ethnic democracy because of the contrast between its racial policy and that followed by most other modern nations. In many countries even organized Christianity has been affected in such a way by racial interests or by the national or class element in race discrimination that one is led to regard the attitude of some Roman Catholic orders that refuse to admit Negroes or mulattoes as distinctly less Christian than the attitude of secular or semi-religious organizations in Brazil that admit coloured persons freely. When C. S. Stewart, an officer in the American Navy, visited Brazil during the middle of the nineteenth century, he was impressed by "the fearfully mongrel aspect" of most of the population; but at the same time a Portuguese institution that has flourished in America since the early days of the colonization of Brazil, the *Misericordia*, made him an admirer of race tolerance as he saw it practised in the Brazilian Empire. Stewart pointed out the fact that the doors of the *Misericordia* hospitals in Rio were open at all hours, night and day, to the sick of both sexes, of all religions, and of every country and colour, without any form or condition of admittance.[1] In qualification of Stewart's praise of Brazilian tolerance one must admit that until a comparatively recent date Brazilians were famous for their intolerance in regard to burial places: not only pagan or unbaptized Negroes but Protestant Europeans and Americans were denied the right to be buried in the so-called sacred or holy cemeteries, the official ones. But this particular intolerance affected only the dead.

Some modern students of race policies think that the Soviet theory of equal opportunity for men of all races goes farther than most Christian agencies in removing not only the psychological and emotional causes of race conflicts but also their economic roots. This is the view of Professor Hans Kohn, an authority on the subject, who writes also that the Soviet Union is now the only large area inhabited by many races that is free, as far as governmental agencies are concerned, of any form of race prejudice; the only one where "the rational belief in the complete equality of all races has become the

1. *Brazil and La Plata: The Personal Record of a Cruise* (New York, 1856), pp. 228–229.

official creed, and energetic educational efforts are being made to raise the social and economic conditions of the underprivileged races." ² I have not visited the Soviet Union and cannot confirm Professor Kohn's statements. But I do know that Brazil, though far from being entirely free of race prejudice, has a number of official, semi-official, and private institutions more advanced than some Christian organizations in dealing with problems of racial relations in a democratic and Christian way.

So general is this liberal attitude in Brazil that international policy is bound to be conditioned by it: if not always through the initiative of official leaders and conventional diplomats, at least under the pressure of its non-official but effective intellectual leaders, whose influence is growing every day, both among the popular elements that form basic Brazilian public opinion and among the intellectual youth and the intelligentsia. In the matter of attitudes towards race-relations problems, no more natural ally of the Soviet Union is to be found among the most powerful nations of America than Brazil. And considering, as we should consider, the increasing importance of such problems in international life and in the field of inter-human relations, we may readily anticipate that such solidarity will be more than a vaguely humanitarian one; it will probably be the basis for common action or common initiative in the field of

2. "Race Conflict," *Encyclopedia of the Social Sciences*, XIII, 40. See also Hans Kohn's *Orient and Occident* (New York, 1934) and Paul Lewinson, *Race, Class and Party* (London, 1932).

international law, where Russia and Brazil will have a right to suggest important changes in attitudes and practices. Their suggestions will be based, not on vague or purely sentimental theories, but on the concrete experience of each of the two communities as areas almost free, or increasingly free, of race prejudice, race conflict, and race discrimination.

The Soviet Union and Brazil, though fundamentally different in their conceptions of social and economic organization, will probably join in the near future as leaders of a movement towards making of racial equality an international issue similar to the one that united such different communities as China and Japan in 1919. As we are reminded by a historian of international relations: "On only one issue debated at Paris [in 1919] were the Chinese and Japanese of one mind and that was on the proposal to amend the League of Nations Covenant so as to recognize racial equality. France and Italy acted in favor of the measure, but Britain, Australia and New Zealand were bitterly opposed. The proposal was adopted by a vote of eleven to six with Wilson and Colonel House not voting; but Wilson, who was presiding, ruled that it was not effective because the vote was not unanimous."[3] Whatever Wilson's motives, Japan blamed him and grew bitter against the United States. In Brazil, the decision had little repercussion at the time and hardly affected Wilson's enormous popularity. But Brazil is becoming increasingly conscious of the fact that its mixed population gives its people a feeling of

3. Hallett Abend, *Treaty Ports* (New York, 1944), p. 242.

unusual solidarity with Asiatic, African, and Indo-Hispanic nations.

At present, Brazil occupies a more important place in the international scene than it did in 1919. Since that year its intellectual as well as economic development has been considerable: its writers, artists, and scientists are now freer to express—sometimes to glorify—the non-European or non-white aspects of Brazilian culture. This change means that Brazil will probably take a leading role in promulgating the racial-equality principle.

There is one request already anticipated from China: that the future world-security organization acknowledge the doctrine of racial equality. And Russia is constantly agitating the racial-equality issue. Speaking to Mexicans, the late Soviet Ambassador to Mexico, Constantin A. Oumansky, pointed out recently that in war and peace Stalin has put foremost "the abolition of racial discrimination"; and also that, at the Moscow Conference of the three powers, Stalin projected into Russian foreign policy a principle already established in the Russian constitution: the abolition of racial discrimination.

At the time of Ambassador Oumansky's remarks, Mr. Carleton Beals, well-known American student of Latin American affairs, was told by a high Mexican foreign-affairs official—a fervent admirer of the United States—that because of American racial discrimination, "so greatly feared in Latin America, and because of our [United States] support of dictatorships, we were on the way to losing our moral and political leadership in the countries to the south of us; that the people and governments would turn more and more to the Soviet Union." [4] This is precisely what is happening. Disappointed liberals of Latin America—in the face of a United States foreign policy that they believe to be as definite in its support of Franco's Spain as that of the most conservative Tories of Great Britain, and equally undemocratic in its attitude on the racial-equality issue —are leaning towards the British Socialists and particularly towards Russia, now considered by them (perhaps with some naïveté) the same messianic nation as the France of the French Revolution was for their eighteenth-century ancestors and as the United States of Washington, Jefferson, and Woodrow Wilson was to Latin American idealists of the early nineteenth century and of twenty-five years ago.

An American expert on international affairs wrote recently (*Time*, November 13, 1944) that there is scarcely a country in the world today where Russia's influence is not on the march. According to him there is only one way in which the Western nations, for whom even an economically secure life without political liberty is not worth living, can meet this challenge: by freeing themselves from want, fear, and suffering while remaining free politically. This would be the ideal solution for Latin Americans, who are still fundamentally Hispanic in their love of personal dignity and freedom

---

4. See Carleton Beals, "The Soviet Wooing of Latin America," *Harper's Magazine*, August, 1944, p. 212.

and in their distaste for rigid regimentation. But their disappointment with Anglo-Saxon liberalism is increasingly bitter. This explains why, with France reduced to a second-rate nation and Spain paralyzed by a semi-Fascist regime, some of them look to Russia as to a messianic nation. Even Catholic priests are taking this attitude; the Bishop of Maura is one of them.

Brazilians have a way of expressing their political or ideological leanings in the names they give their children. There was a time when children were named for saints of the Catholic calendar and from sacred history. Then came the independence movement, and children were given Amerindian names. Still later, they were called after French, Spanish, and Spanish American revolutionary or romantic heroes: Ubirajara, Danton, Lamartine, Lafayette, Benjamin Constant, Chateaubriand, Cid, Bolívar. (I had a great-great-uncle whose name, instead of being that of a Portuguese saint, was "Voltaire.") Then came another phase: names were taken from Greek literature and Roman history—a phase that corresponded to the reign of Dom Pedro II, a good man but a somewhat pedantic student of the classics. With the Republican movement, anti-monarchical and extremely liberal parents began to give their children names taken from British and United States history: Milton, Newton, Washington, Jefferson, Lincoln, Gladstone, Franklin. Some anti-clerical parents went so far as to name their children after Luther and Calvin. Juarez was a name given to many. And soon after the First World War numerous Brazilian children were given the name of Wilson. It is significant that at present there is a tendency among some Brazilian parents to choose names from Russian novels and Russian history.

There seems to be no doubt that Russia's standing on the race issue is fascinating to liberal and perhaps naïve Brazilians, while the United States prejudice against the half-breed continues to be an obstacle to the development of really friendly relations between the two peoples. Some years ago a Yale professor, Hiram Bingham, wrote that the fundamental difference in racial attitude between the average Anglo-Saxon American and the average Latin American made it difficult for the Anglo-Saxon Americans "to treat fairly" with their Southern neighbours.[5] This difficulty has not entirely disappeared with the "Good Neighbor" policy and it will be probably used against the United States by clever Russian diplomats and even by shrewd Britons if power politics continues to dominate international relations, with Latin America as one of the best markets for imperial, if not imperialistic, nations during the next decades.

Some students of international affairs think that instead of sending to countries like Brazil diplomats of the conventional type who associate only with men in power, church authorities, and elegant society lions, the United States Government would be wise to appoint men who could acquaint Brazilians with the work done in this country for more democratic racial relations—men familiar with the activities of the Council against

5. *The Monroe Doctrine* (New Haven, 1915), p. 24.

Intolerance in America, the Council on Intercultural Relations, the Bureau of Intercultural Education, the National Association for the Advancement of Colored People, the Federal Council of Churches of Christ in America, the National Conference of Christians and Jews, the National Maritime Union, the Fair Employment Practices Committee, and the Bureau of Indian Affairs. Very few Brazilians know anything about the splendid work being done by liberal and Christian leaders in this country for more democratic relations between whites and Indians, whites and Orientals, whites and Negroes; they hear more about ethnic democracy in Russia.

The results of a policy of race equality such as is followed in modern Russia, or of approximate race equality such as has long been practised in Brazil, do not seem to confirm the fears of those who speak or write of mongrelization as a biological catastrophe. On the contrary, the evidence appears to favour those who describe the results of miscegenation as even aesthetically attractive. The theorists of "racial integrity" need to revamp their arguments against race mixture or to invent new ones. The Russians, a large number of whom are mixed-bloods, are certainly far from being debased or decadent peoples, or "passive," "feminine races," as some prejudiced anthropologists and sociologists of the nineteenth century called them. Look at statements like these: "The Russians, with their strong infusion of Mongoloid blood, excel rather in suffering and endurance than in action that brings freedom" (Fritz Lentz); or "The

Russian folk ... is by temperament passive, rather gentle, ready to obey, feminine rather than masculine in character" (F. R. Radosavlevich); or "The European stocks with a strong infusion of mongoloid blood have a rather heavy mentality; they cling to the traditional," and "advanced technical methods are much weaker there than in the regions where the nordic race predominates" (Lentz). In recent years such statements have been applied oftener to countries like Brazil than to Russia. But Brazil's development has already begun to refute those generalizations. Nor are the Mexican people, likewise mixed-bloods, regarded by modern anthropologists as "passive," as they were by critics in the days of the Díaz dictatorship.

Not all German, English, and American scientists who have been to Brazil have been so pessimistic over "the fearfully mongrel aspect of most of the population" as was the French diplomat and littérateur Count de Gobineau or the American Navy officer C. S. Stewart. The most authoritative ones, in point of scientific training and sociological vision—men like von Martius in the early nineteenth century, Alfred Russel Wallace, Bates, and Professor Konrad Guenther, not to mention specialists on race mixture like Professors Rüdiger Bilden and Donald Pierson—have written almost enthusiastically about the social and aesthetic results of race amalgamation in Brazil. "Mongoloid" or "Negroid" Brazil is credited with creativeness in more than one field of artistic and technical activity; it is being praised also for its traditional race tolerance.

One of the most intelligent travellers who visited Brazil during the first half of the nineteenth century was an American, the Rev. Walter Colton, U.S.N. He noticed in relation to the African slaves that "their freedom in many cases lies within their reach and may be obtained, as it often is, by industry and frugality." He also observed: "When free, he [the slave] goes to the ballot-box, and is eligible to a seat in the national legislature. Nor would anybody here go into hysterics should he marry a woman whose skin should be a shade whiter than his own. It is for us Americans to preach up humanity, freedom and equality and then turn up our blessed noses if an African takes a seat at the same table on board a steamboat. The misery is that they who preach equality the loudest are generally the last to practice it."[6] Two other American divines who visited Brazil during the reign of Dom Pedro II reacted in the same way to the ethnically democratic situation they found there; I refer to J. C. Fletcher and D. P. Kidder, authors of *Brazil and the Brazilians*. The Rev. Mr. Fletcher wrote: "Some of the most intelligent men that I have met with in Brazil—men educated at Paris and Coimbra—were of African descent, whose ancestors were slaves. Thus, if a man has freedom, money and merit, no matter how black may be his skin, no place in society is refused him. It is surprising also to observe the ambition and the advancement of some of these men with negro blood in their veins." Though he admitted a certain, though by no means strong, prejudice in favour of men of pure

6. *Deck and Port* (New York, 1850), pp. 112–113.

white descent, he pointed out that in the colleges, and in the medical, law, and theological schools, there was no distinction of colour.[7]

I have already mentioned the book written twenty years ago by a scientifically trained American, Mr. Roy Nash, as one of the best ever published about Brazil. Referring to the miscegenation process, he says that it "has not gone so far in Brazil that there are not still large numbers of unmixed Portuguese, Indians and Negroes, still some consciousness of color and even more of caste; but it has gone so far that one may expect its completion perhaps within five or six generations." [8] The question: "Does Brazil's four hundred years of history prove that the admixture of widely different stocks spells degeneration?" is emphatically answered by the American author: "By no manner of means. The indictment of a ruling class, of an economic system, of a false philosophy is not the indictment of a people. . . . Many are the Brazilians who know better than I that . . . of the hardburnt bricks of freely cooperating labor, public health and popular education must be built the Brazil of the Future." [9]

This is also the view of able and conscientious Brazilian students of the social history and the ethnic and social conditions of their country like Roquette Pinto. They have pointed out, in sociological essays and anthropological works, the pressing need for Brazil's pur-

7. *Brazil and the Brazilians* (Boston, 1879), p. 133.
8. Nash, *op. cit.*, p. 60.
9. *Ibid.*, pp. 356–357.

suing a policy of social recuperation. Regions where slavery has been for centuries the dominant system of social organization are like areas that have suffered devastation in long or successive wars: they need social recuperation, not the replacement of the mestizo population by an "Aryan" one.

Brazil's foreign policy is bound to be increasingly affected by the progressive change in the economic basis of its social structure from slavery and a semi-feudal regime of one-crop agriculture and latifundium to an economically and socially democratic regime marked by diversification of crops and fragmentation of large estates. This change is enabling Brazil to attract the best type of immigrants instead of being forced to look to Chinese coolies as substitutes for slave labour. It also makes it possible for Brazilians to raise the standards of living of those descendants of Indians, Negroes, and Europeans who have remained ill fed and almost orientally poor, as well as landless, in a country famous for its immensely large and undeveloped estates and extensive unoccupied land. It seems to anthropologists and sociologists who know Brazil well that the poor or miserable part of the Brazilian population, whether wholly white or mestizo, needs only to be given better opportunities to reveal its capacity and strength. After his contact with the Brazilians of central Brazil, Theodore Roosevelt wrote that the "endurance and the bull-like strength" of the men of the Brazilian common people whom he knew, as well as the "intelligence" of the officers of the Brazilian army with whom he travelled—most of them men of mixed blood—made him "wonder at the ignorance of those who do not realize the energy and power that are so often possessed by, and that may be so readily developed in the men of the tropics." [10]

Few responsible Brazilians, particularly those of the younger generation, have any doubts concerning the energy and capacity of their landless and diseased fellow countrymen who have not been given a real opportunity to develop their qualities and to become efficient contributors to the growth of Brazil. Actually there are many who consider the integration of these men in the community as a creative element in it as more important than the attracting of immigrants to Brazil. Both problems—that of developing native man-power through education, sanitation, and the democratizing of land ownership and of attracting immigrants—make it imperative that Brazil adopt an increasingly democratic attitude in regard to human relations at home and relations with foreign countries.

Brazilian foreign policy is conditioned by the fact that Brazil, now in a phase of industrialization, mechanizing of agriculture, and scientific colonizing of areas like the Amazon, needs immigrants. But not only is the foreign policy affected by such a need; its domestic policy also is concerned, since no colonization of Brazil by freemen is possible without a more democratic disposition of public lands.

Lord Bryce regretted the absence from Brazil, as well as from the other South American countries he

10. *Through the Brazilian Wilderness* (New York, 1914), p. 254.

visited more than thirty years ago, of small land-owners whose interest in good administration would be intelligent and strong enough to rouse them to their civic duty.[11] Only in certain areas of southern Brazil is a development of this sort taking place. In this connection one aspect of the problem should again be pointed out: in the colonization of most areas of northern and central Brazil it will be impossible for the pioneering immigrants really to succeed as individuals. Enlarging the tradition of the *Bandeiras*, they will have to be organized in co-operative groups and protected by the Brazilian Government or by special organizations.

As individuals the Brazilians from the North-east who have gone to the Amazon area have been heroic. Some of them have done wonders for the colonization of that area. But little can be accomplished in this way. The Brazilian colonization of the Amazon will probably have to be a co-operative task in which the army will find an opportunity to do an even greater work in promoting large-scale sanitation of a tropical region than the one the United States Army did in Panama.

Some Brazilians have been insisting on the employment of the Army, when it is not engaged in national defence, in contributing to public works; for instance, in the construction of railways, which serve both a strategic and an economic and cultural purpose. This is an old French idea not very well received by French orthodox advocates of an army for strictly military purposes only; nevertheless a Frenchman was bold enough

11. Bryce, *op. cit.*, p. 537.

to suggest, years ago, that if the nation co-operates with the army in time of war, it is but just that the army should assist the nation in time of peace. To a certain extent this has been done in Brazil. Many Americans have heard of the remarkable work of General Rondon and other officers of the Brazilian army among the savage tribes of central Brazil and in the construction of railroads and telegraph lines in that part of the country. Work of this sort may be accomplished on a larger scale by the Brazilian army in the Amazon area, whose colonization is too tremendous a task to be accomplished by individuals.

The idea of a semi-military development of a region is not original with the suggestion that the Amazon be thus colonized. More than half a century ago a Brazilian, Henrique Velloso de Oliveira, presented a plan for the colonization by "industrial armies" both of old areas dominated for centuries by feudal land-owners and of virgin lands. The members of the so-called "industrial armies," instead of acting like individual pioneers, would act under a plan. Co-operation would be their method; diversification of agriculture would be developed; and pioneering activities would be stimulated.

The basic element of such "industrial armies" would be Brazilian young men. But to them would be added, as soon as prosperity came to them, European colonists. A number of European girls would be imported to be the wives of the successful or prosperous Brazilian members of the "industrial armies" who would prefer to marry blondes. Among the Brazilians there would be white descendants of Europeans, but also a large number of mixed-bloods. Portuguese, Spanish, Italian, and even German immigrants, male and female, have not hesitated to marry Brazilians of Indian and Negro origin; and in view of this fact it would be easy to develop ethnic democracy among the "industrial armies."

It seems to me unfortunate that Oliveira's plan was never put in practice. Probably it would have solved some of the problems connected with the European colonization of Brazil, especially that of the democratic disposition or redistribution of public and feudal lands. As I said before, this problem remains a serious one to be faced by Brazil before good European peasants and agriculturists come there to establish themselves as farmers free from strict control of agencies of their own governments such as the Japanese and also some European groups have had. Control of immigrants is the Brazilian Government's business, though agreements may be reached through which European or other governments may be allowed the right to have their representatives act, not as supervisors, but as advisers to and collaborators with the Brazilian Government concerning migration problems of common interest.

Brazilian foreign policy will be influenced for a long time by Brazil's relations with those countries that are likely to continue to enrich Portuguese America with their blood, their human values, and the work of their peasants, labourers, and artisans; for Brazil needs immigrants. To meet this need, it is the hope of Brazil to receive from the various countries of Europe a large number of agricultural and industrial workers. Some students of the subject think that the Italian farmer fits into the Brazilian way of life especially well. But it is to the political as well as the economic and cultural interest of Brazil to receive as many agricultural immigrants from Portugal as possible; they and the Spaniards are the type basically needed.

Brazil's foreign policy will be greatly affected—is being affected already—by the rapid industrial development of the country. Portuguese America is said to be ready to produce all the steel that she needs for her own use and eventually some to be exported. This portends an important change in the country's economic as well as political life and relations. From the point of view of an international policy, diversification of production and industrialization mean that Brazilian economy is ceasing to be passive or semi-colonial. As Mr. Normano points out so well in his *Brazil: A Study of Economic Types:* "the monoproductive character of Brazilian economy has made the country a captive of world prices," and "the change in the leading products influences not only national but international politics too. . . . The chief market for sugar, gold and cotton was Europe. Rubber and coffee were the bridge to the United States." [12] But with the development of industries, Brazilian economy is becoming an active one. This

12. Pp. 55–56.

means a greater independence in its political attitudes, and the end, or the beginning of the end, of semi-colonialism.

Through the expansion of its textile industry Brazil is also becoming a great exporter of cotton cloth to other Latin American nations. Some of it is made in response to the need for adapting wearing apparel to a tropical climate and according to the standards of taste prevailing in a large part of the Brazilian population and an equally large part of the Spanish—especially Spanish Indo-American—population. But most of the Brazilian cotton and silk products are sold today in the Latin American republics lying in the temperate zone. This fact means another transformation in Brazilian economic life and economic relations, for this widening of trade is stimulating the development in Latin America of what someone has called "a mutual discovery phase."

Closer relations between Brazil and the other American republics and between Brazil and Portuguese Africa, Portuguese Asia, the Cape Verde Islands, the Azores, Madeira, and Portugal will probably result from the conversion of present military airports in Brazil to commercial use. Brazil already has a factory for airplane motors. Because of the development of industrial areas, its many and valuable resources, and its technical as well as intellectual progress, Brazil is in many important respects becoming the leader of the entire Portuguese-speaking world. This world may soon become a federation with a common citizenship and a number of other common rights and responsibilities. Reciprocal duties will then be involved. It is interesting to note the growing tendency of the new generations in Portuguese Africa, in the Cape Verde Islands, and, to a lesser extent, in the Azores, to follow inspirations and suggestions from Brazil. The new Brazilian literature and art, and recent advances in social and scientific studies in Brazil under intellectual leaders and through the use of methods more daring, aggressive, and modern than those known in Portugal, seem to be affecting the traditional system of inter-relations in the Portuguese-speaking world in such a way that Brazil is becoming the intellectual, artistic, and scientific centre of that world. Julio Dantas, a distinguished Portuguese intellectual, has said that the best writers of the Portuguese language are now in Brazil; this is also the opinion of other Portuguese critics. And some of the most prominent Portuguese scholars are now established in Brazil, where they teach, or write, or have their books published. Nevertheless Portugal remains the reservoir of many ancestral or traditional values that none of its former colonies is able to produce, not even mature Brazil.

Brazilian foreign policy is conditioned also by the geographical situation of Brazil as an American nation. We may be in the first phase of development of another federation of which Brazil is as natural a member as of a Portuguese-speaking one—a Pan American federation. The two federations, if they develop, may become sub-federations in regard to a larger one: an Atlantic Federation, in which the place to be occupied by Brazil will be determined by its geography and by its history.

From the point of view of plant or animal ecology, South America may be one continent, North America another. From the point of view of human ecology, Latin America may be one continent, Anglo-Saxon America another. But from a broader point of view that takes into consideration all aspects of interdependence among the American nations—interdependence in both physical and social space and relations—the American continent is increasingly one continent. As such it needs a combined continental policy in which variety is not disregarded for the sake of an excessive uniformity. The American nations seem to have common enemies. All the evidence leads us to believe that a Japanese or German feudal imperialism would be far less tolerant of an ethnically and culturally free and democratic development in Latin America than British or Anglo-American bourgeois imperialism is or has been. With all their imperfections, Britain and the United States are constantly improving or seeking to improve their politically democratic systems or, rather, their methods of dealing with inter-human relations and human differences.

Latin American nations came into existence through a widespread revolt against European autocratic systems of repressing human and cultural differences and of exploiting human labour. Their political independence sprang from a revolt whose motive was similar to that of the American Revolution: taxation without representation. They separated from Spain and Portugal because they were being exploited and at the same time repressed—intellectually, economically, and politically

Foreign Policy

repressed by narrow Portuguese and Spanish politicians.

Since its first attempts to become an independent nation, Brazil has looked for a defensive and offensive alliance with the United States, against Portuguese threats of reconquest. The first Brazilian *chargé d'affaires* in the United States went so far as to propose an alliance between Brazil and the United States "in order to resist European interference in case Portugal called a partner to her assistance." [13] Even before that, during Brazil's attempt in 1817 to separate from Portugal through a romantic and unsuccessful republican revolution, the rebels of Pernambuco tried to secure the aid of the United States for their cause. And as far back as the eighteenth century, the rebels of Minas Geraes tried unsuccessfully, through a Brazilian student in France named Maia, to interest Thomas Jefferson in that first effort towards Brazilian independence. According to Oliveira Lima, the appeal addressed from Philadelphia to the President of the United States by that plenipotentiary *in partibus* of the Brazilian Republicans of 1817 contained the essential principles of Pan-Americanism in an empirical form, just as Bolívar's plan for an American union was its "scientific conception." Perhaps the failure of the Brazilian Republicans of 1817 to obtain the help of the United States was in part due to the fact that they sent a coloured man as their emissary.

It was not until 1857 that the idea of an alliance of the United States with Brazil was officially considered from

13. Oliveira Lima, "Brazil's Foreign Policy" (a lecture given at Williamstown, August, 1922, ms.).

a United States point of view. The American minister in Rio, Richard Kidder Meade, in a speech presenting his credentials to the Emperor Dom Pedro II, said then that "such an alliance will ensure for mutual defense a unity of action and feeling that will prove invincible in the future." Since that year, however, the idea of a political alliance has disappeared under a broader conception of inter-American relations: the so-called "scientific conception" of Pan-Americanism first outlined by Bolívar. But the fact remains that both similarities and differences attract Brazil to the United States in a special way and make the two countries particularly complementary to each other.

From a purely social point of view, such have been the changes for the better in the relations between the two countries that today even a coloured man, if sent as emissary from Brazil to the United States, would probably find a decent (if not warm) reception in this country, at least among the best-educated Americans. The point is important: a changed attitude towards men of coloured races seems to some students of inter-American relations essential to the development of Pan-Americanism if the latter is to mean real reciprocity and effective mutual respect. One should not forget that the commercial success of the Germans in Brazil before 1914 was largely due to the fact that, more than the Anglo-Saxons, they were then socially democratic in Latin America. For, though some Germans in Brazil have married into old white or white-Indian families, a number of them—like a number of Portuguese, Italian,

Spanish, and French—have married beautiful mulatto, quadroon, or octoroon girls. I do not mean that racial intermarriage is a necessary pre-requisite to a vital or honest Pan-Americanism. I do not mean that every American, North and South, should marry outside his racial class in order to be a good Pan-American. Far from it. International and inter-racial marriages are always adventures, just as it is an adventure, in the present social organization of our Western civilization, for a man to marry a woman palpably below his own rank in life. One disagreeable consequence may be a domestic conflict of cultures, with the mother-in-law playing an important role. But in democratic America colour or race should not in itself taboo such adventures—too many individuals have made a success of it. No man ever had a more devoted and understanding wife than the Brazilian psychiatrist Juliano Moreira, who was a very dark Negro; she was a German. And other such cases might be mentioned.

Reciprocity and mutual respect seem to me an essential basis for developing really friendly inter-American relations. This mutual respect should take into consideration the fact that a democratic tradition is common to all Americans, Latin and Anglo-Saxon. The Latins have developed the ethnic aspect of democracy more than the political, and the Anglo-Saxons the purely political aspect more than the ethnic. If they are to become really good neighbours and increasingly democratic in their organization and culture, Latin and Anglo-Saxon Americans will probably enrich each other with the best results of their special cultural developments. But it would be a sociological error to work for uniformity in the American continent, instead of for unity combined with variety—though the respect for variety should not go so far as to include tolerance of such undemocratic institutions as *caudillismo* and lynching, anti-Semitism and the Ku Klux Klan.

Though the static part of the Brazilian masses, still influenced by four long centuries of life and work under slavery, tend to tolerate the despotic paternalism of *caudillos,* there is a dynamic part of the same masses whose eagerness to rise socially and culturally and to improve their material and intellectual conditions of living manifests itself in the opposite direction: as a constant revolt against autocratic or despotic paternalism. This is also the attitude of most of the Brazilians who are the descendants of the old master class; they, too, are opposed to *caudillismo.* Some of them may be inclined—this is another story—to forms of government more like the British than any other, in their combination of aristocratic control of public affairs with democratic opportunity open to all who are capable of participating in that control.

Foreign observers who generalize about Brazil, taking into consideration only the politically dead or inarticulate part of its people, seem too hasty in their conclusions in favour of strongly paternalistic regimes for Portuguese America, as well as for other parts. Centuries before Fascism and Nazism rose in Europe, Brazil tasted the good, as well as the evil, of a quasi Fascist or quasi

Nazist regime. I mean the Jesuit missions. It is well known that the Jesuits exercised a benevolent paternalistic control over large groups of Indians of Brazil and Paraguay. How perfect this technique was is illustrated by their way of setting up a large wooden image of some terrible-looking saint, inside of which a man (a Jesuit) was introduced, to tell the Indians what they must do. I have seen some of these old images in Rio Grande do Sul; a child should not see them, lest he develop deep neurotic fears. But nobody can deny that in Brazil, as in Paraguay, the Jesuits were efficient administrators who developed agriculture and industry in their missions, introduced new plants, and had every detail in the daily life of every mission Indian under their paternalistic discipline. Professor Walter Goetz writes of the Jesuit "state" of Paraguay—which had an extension in southern Brazil—that "it was a virtual autocracy, controlling the native population by communistic economic and social regulations." [14] He adds: "That the natives received good treatment from the Jesuits is beyond doubt." But it was the sort of "good treatment" that tends to keep a human group mere children. The same efficiency, as far as material prosperity is concerned, is recognized by another authoritative student of the subject, José Ots y Capdequi. But he thinks that "the mission regime made impossible the development of a self-reliant personality." [15] The mission regime was also imperialistic in its lack of faith in the native; its organ-

14. "Jesuits," *Encyclopedia of the Social Sciences*, VIII, 388.
15. "Native Policy," *Encyclopedia of the Social Sciences*, XI, 259.

izers seem to have had little confidence in the capacity of the natives and of the descendants of the Spanish and Portuguese settlers of America, both creole and mixed-blood, to develop cultural autonomy and political self-government.

If one goes today to the part of Brazil that came under the most direct control of the Jesuits, one finds among the descendants of the mission Indians, not pleasant recollections of that paternalistic regime, but hatred towards the well-meaning but autocratic missionaries. I do not know of any Brazilian from that area who has the slightest enthusiasm for the once theocratic lords of the Rio Grande do Sul missions. There is nothing like the tolerant feeling towards benevolent paternalism that one finds among a large number of descendants of plantation slaves in the northern provinces of Brazil. On the contrary, it seems that the war-cry of seventeenth-century Indians against the Jesuits of the "reduçoes" expressed what is still the core idea in the revolt of their descendants against autocratic control of their lives: "Me mata mas não me reduz" (You kill me but you will not "reduce" me).

With such traditions alive in Brazil—alive among the most dynamic groups of its population, both educated and illiterate—it is possible to conclude that this country is among the modern communities inclined to democracy; inclined to democracy, not only through the socially and ethnically democratic process of race amalgamation and cultural interpenetration that has been active among its people, but also through the eagerness of many Brazilians for forms of government in which the development of human personality is not neglected. It appears that the Brazilian ideal of human happiness (an ideal affected by many traditions and tendencies of its intelligentsia and its common people alike) does not stop at material gains or conveniences; it includes the development of human personality in ways that seem to have been accentuated through the wide exchange of intellectual and moral values made possible by democratic contact between various races and cultures.

It seems that Brazil has a distinct contribution to make to the development of human personality in the modern world. The contribution will probably come from the extra-European type of civilization that the most dynamic and creative groups of the Brazilian population are developing in spite of immense difficulties. It will manifest itself through the inter-American and foreign policy of Brazil as well as through all authentically Brazilian art and literature. But the policy, the art, and the literature will be hypocritical whenever Brazil seeks to express herself intellectually and politically as an altogether white nation; whenever she acts as if her interests, her problems, and her ideals were those of a European or sub-European nation and not those of a really new and dynamic American community, not ashamed of its Amerindian, Jewish, and African basic elements but proud of them.

Three years ago I visited Argentina, Uruguay, and Paraguay, and in each of these countries—especially in the first—I found that, in spite of the fact that the majority of the people and the best elements in the press were and are friendly towards us, there was a well-prepared movement against Brazil that reminded me of similar agitations cleverly prepared by German secret agents in the Balkans: movements characterized by the same technique of psychological war. The agitation in Argentina against Brazil in the late 'thirties and the early 'forties (possibly by Nazi agents) took the colour of a nationalistic movement in favour of a great Argentine figure of the past—the dictator Rosas—presented to the popular mind as a powerful and brave enemy of "Jews" and "Brazilian mulattoes." According to the legend, "Brazilian mulatto diplomats," through shrewd diplomacy, had robbed Argentina of lands that rightly belonged to the Argentine "white people." The note of race hatred is present in a most characteristic way in the pro-Rosas, pro-Fascist, anti-democratic and anti-Brazilian movement in Argentina, a movement whose main purpose is evidently to divide the people of Argentina from the people of Brazil.

Such general remarks about there being mulattoes in Brazil, as well as specific statements about specific Brazilian mulattoes who in the Empire and the Republic have been responsible for Brazilian national and international policy, still trouble some sensitive Brazilians—fifty-, sixty-, and seventy-year-old Brazilians. But they do not disturb the majority of the young generation, who are practically free from morbid sensitiveness about the fact that Brazil has a mixed-blood population. So strong are the evidences of a capacity to build a new and original civilization in America already given by Brazilians of the most diverse ethnic origins that young Brazilians, facing truth as it is being revealed to them by historians, anthropologists, and sociologists who have ceased to be sub-European in their outlook and have become American in the best sense of the word, are proud of their mestizo heroes, their mestizo composers, their mestizo statesmen, their mestizo writers, artists, industrial leaders, inventors, scientists, and administrators. And they could remind the Argentine race purists that a great statesman of nineteenth-century Argentina was a mulatto, and that Manuel Ugarte, the famous writer, was also a mulatto.

As I pointed out before, under the monarchical regime in the nineteenth century any Brazilian, no matter what his origin, race, or colour, could become prime minister and lead the country if he was a man of exceptional talent or personality. During the Republic it has been perfectly natural to see a man like Nilo Peçanha, a mulatto of very humble origin, succeed, as Minister of Foreign Affairs, Lauro Müller, the blue-eyed and purely "Aryan" son of a German colonist of Santa Catharina province. Brazilian race purists are today a very small and almost ridiculous group.

Young Brazilians consider it more and more their duty to oppose all forms of race snobbery which might prevent Brazil and the population of Portuguese-speaking areas culturally led today by Brazil from carrying on their vast experiment in ethnical and social democratization. In this connection it is instructive to note that even the Brazilian quasi Nazist or quasi Fascist organization—the so-called "Integralismo"—did not lift its voice officially against those who favour the incorporation of all race elements into the Brazilian community—a fact that suggests the strength of that tendency. Hence the remark of Professor Lewis Hanke that Nazi racial ideas can expect only opposition from the Latin American cultural fusionists, and what is more important, that "this group—the fusionist—is more nobly nationalistic than any other in Latin America."

Fusionism being the dominant policy in Brazil, that nation is out of harmony with European or sub-European white nations every time they speak or act as European or sub-European powers and look down upon non-European nations. But she is also out of place among predominantly coloured communities whose race consciousness is stronger than their national consciousness. Owing to the possibilities for social improvement and cultural expression, there never was any chance for the Brazilian descendants of Africans to develop that consciousness of being a Negro which exists in the United States even in individuals of distant or remote African blood and of physical characteristics clearly acceptable according to Graeco-Roman and Nordic aesthetic standards.

VI

THE MODERN LITERATURE OF BRAZIL: ITS RELATION TO BRAZILIAN SOCIAL PROBLEMS

LITERATURE and art are not the field of the literary or art critic only; they are also the concern of the sociologist, of the social historian or anthropologist, and of the social psychologist. For through literature and art men seem to reveal their personality and, when there is one, their national ethos. Through the arts they describe the most crushing social conditions and breathe their most revolutionary wishes. And through the arts they portray the particularly oppressed as well as the most vigorously dynamic aspects of their personality and their national ethos.

For a long time Brazilian art and literature remained almost inarticulate and passively colonial or sub-European. Aleijadinho, the mulatto sculptor of eighteenth-century colonial churches in the gold-mine region of Brazil, was one of the few artists to appear with a socially significant artistic message and a technique distinguished by creativeness, audacity, and non-European characteristics in a century marked, in Brazil, by academic literature and imitative art. Aleijadinho, the son of a Portuguese artisan and a Negro woman, was born under the shadow of slavery; and a terrible disease that ate most of his fingers seems to have increased his consciousness of belonging to an outcast part of the population and his tendency to social revolt. He worked assisted by loyal slaves. It is easy to see how significant were the material and social conditions that favoured the technically non-European and sometimes socially anti-European qualities in his sculptures. If I rightly interpret his work, it was and remains an expression of social revolt and of the Brazilian native and mestizo wish for independence from white or European masters and exploiters of slave labour.

Religious art was his medium of expression. Sometimes, as I look at his work, it seems to reveal very clearly his conscious or unconscious identification on the one hand, as a highly sensitive and potentially revolutionary mulatto, with Christ and the primitive Christian martyrs (masochism), and, on the other hand, with the most terrific Old Testament prophets who preached against social sins and made personal sinners suffer mentally, if not physically (sadism). His satirical or sarcastic way of brutally exaggerating, in the Roman officers and soldiers and in the Jewish high priests who persecuted Jesus, their noses and other racial characteristics seems to be also an expression of his revolt against the domination and exploitation of a rich country like the gold-mine region of Brazil by arrogant Portuguese officers and soldiers and, according to some students of the period, by priests and friars as well as by Jewish merchants at-

Modern Literature 157

tracted to that part of Brazil by the presence of gold and diamonds. In Minas Geraes, on account of the large profits from the gold mines, there was, beginning in the seventeenth century, a particularly dramatic rivalry between the Portuguese of Portugal (a large number of whom in the eighteenth century were arrogant officers and soldiers) and native Brazilians, some of whom were mestizos of white and Indian, and, later, mulattoes. For the slave population in that region rapidly became one of the largest in Portuguese America.

It is also to be noted that in the gold-mine region relations between master and slaves were, from the beginning, different from what they were in the plantation region: less patriarchal, more impersonal, and (according to reports from travellers and from other sources) more cruel.

Aleijadinho was a natural, if not a logical, product of his region. In all his work there seems to be a symbolic intent, probably well known to some of his contemporaries though it has escaped the notice of most of his critics and interpreters. It seems to me that the sculptor's physical vision was distorted by his desire to convey a political message through a then popular form of art—religious sculpture. If I am right, he was a pioneer; a sort of mulatto El Greco in his daring distortions of the human form, he anticipated by two centuries the work of Rivera and Orozco, of Portinari and Cicero Dias—modern Latin Americans in whose art there is frequently a symbolic political intent, as well as a tendency toward exaggeration, distortion, caricature. He also was a pioneer of the modern literary art of Brazil—the art of novelists like José Lins do Rego, Jorge Amado, and Raquel de Queiroz, to mention only three of the most characteristic ones; the art of poets like Manuel Bandeira, Carlos Drummond de Andrade, Jorge de Lima, Murilo Mendes, Venicius de Morais, and Odorico Tavares, to name six of the most daring in their association of social problems with poetical art and in their eagerness to be the expression of an extra- or ultra-European Brazil rather than merely the colonial echo of a purely European philosophy of life and of a purely European literary or musical technique—an eagerness that is found also in Heitor Villa-Lobos, the Brazilian composer. For although the younger writers of Brazil have grown up under European literary influences and some have imitated, or still imitate, Europeans on the mechanical or technical side of their art, they are powerfully Brazilian in their characterization, exaggeration, and interpretation of life; in their freshness of visional truth and essential (not formal or conventional) fidelity to the living actuality and the living past of Brazil. Some of them are also masters in the style of El Greco: they like distortion of reality when they feel the need to make reality more real or more Brazilian than it appears to be. Such distortions are to be found in some of the pages of Jorge Amado, for instance, where purely visional truth is freely exceeded by the poetic and sometimes political dramatization of situations.

Satire, as well as an interest in social problems and revolt against political abuse, is an early characteristic of

Brazilian literature. Though no viceroy of Brazil, no king, no emperor, no president, no bishop has been assassinated in the history of the country, some have suffered almost the equivalent of death at the hands of literary and popular satirists. As early as 1666 a colonial governor sent to Pernambuco by the King of Portugal was given such a ridiculous nickname and satirized so unmercifully in literary and popular verse and prose for his graft and his incompetence that it was easy for a group of Brazilians to assault him one day, as he was walking through a street, followed by his military aide. They took his spectacularly large sword from him, quietly put him on a ship, and sent him off. This would probably have been impossible if the moustaches he wore—copied from those of a German general of the seventeenth century—had not made him such a perfect butt.

In the same century there lived in Bahia and Pernambuco a brilliant man, Gregorio de Mattos, noted for his satirical talent in verse. More than that, he was a social critic of considerable importance. Some of his verses describing the local types are the work of a master caricaturist and a penetrating social critic. At the same time, he was the first Brazilian poet to interpret the sorrows and joys of Brazilian life in its first phase of transition from almost purely European standards of culture to a mestizan, extra-European culture. There is little pity in his representations of bishops, governors, planters, women, and priests, in whom he always found some human weakness to laugh at. Some of his verses became popular. I think that he should be considered a pioneer of social literature, social art, and social or political caricature in Brazil. From this point of view he was as important as Aleijadinho, the sculptor. Matos was more intellectual, but Aleijadinho had more emotional vigour in his art and more symbolism in his distortions of the human form. The sculptor was probably influenced to a greater extent than Gregorio de Mattos was by popular art and by popular verse, for, as I said above, he was the son of a Negro woman and consequently came into closer contact with the peasants and the slaves than the sophisticated Matos did.

The great popular art in colonial Brazil was that of ex-votos, or votive tablets, hung in the churches, with their naïve exaggeration of miracles—for instance, deliverance from shipwreck. This art was various. Wood, clay, or wax sculptures of heads, torsos, hands, feet, hearts, livers, eyes, and other members were offered to the saints whose help had been asked—effectually—in the cure of this or that infirmity or disease. The burning of the Judases was another aspect of this popular art; the crowd had an opportunity to satirize the un-Christion behaviour of some local lord, represented by a grotesque straw figure of Judas in old clothes. Even native pastry and Brazilian popular confectionery had an element of caricature in them, caricature of such sacred things as rosaries and such respectable beings as nuns. Cakes and sweets had—some of them still have— names that orthodox Catholics of Anglo-Saxon countries would probably consider sacrilegious. *Rosaries* was the name of one, a delicacy mentioned by the American Ewbank in his list of popular articles of native pastry that he knew in Brazil when he was there in the middle of the nineteenth century;[1] *Celestial Slices,* the name of another; and *Angel's Hair,* the name of still another. *Nuns' Bellies,* the name of a fourth one, is a terribly sacrilegious name; so is *Heavenly Bacon,* the name of a light pudding composed of almond paste, eggs, sugar, butter, and a spoonful or two of flour. But sacred and worldly things were mixed in many ways, as if caricature were ubiquitous in Brazilian life. Some of these cakes and sweets with sacrilegious names were made in convents by the nuns themselves. And the venders of confectionery were also the venders of the coarse wooden images of saints. Each of these two arts—confectionery and the sculpture of saints—was a popular art distinguished by caricature. The sculpture of saints tended to exaggerate, distort, and magnify this or that power of the saint, and thus resembled the ex-voto described above. Born under such influences it was natural that Aleijadinho and, to a lesser extent, Gregorio de Mattos should develop into masters of social caricature.

The same tendency is to be found in the songs of the illiterate Brazilians and in popular verse written by popular poets for labourers and peasants who can read only simple words. These songs and poems recount episodes that have made a deep impression upon the popular mind; and they often tend to exaggerate or distort facts and personalities—not in an effort to hide the truth, but

[1] Ewbank, *op. cit.,* p. 136.

rather to make clear, violently and brutally clear, the most important characteristics of a personality or a fact from the point of view of the popular reader or hearer. This, also, is the technique of caricature.

This technique has also marked what there is of a national stage in Brazil: the so-called *revista*. Amazed at the freedom enjoyed by the authors of *revistas* in their bold caricatures of political personages, a foreign observer in Brazil thirty years ago remarked that he supposed that on the stage, as in the Brazilian press, there must be some limit beyond which the libel law became operative, but that he could not imagine where it was drawn—he saw theatre audiences rocking with laughter when well-known political personages were caricatured.

It is a fact—and not a legend—that some Brazilian politicians and even statesmen have considered it a disgrace not to be caricatured in *revistas*, newspaper cartoons, and café stories. One of these, when nothing unpleasant or caustic was being written or said about him, took the trouble himself to write something of that sort about his political ideas or his personality, and sent it under a false name to an opposition paper. Then, and only then, he felt well: he was alive, he said—not harmless.

Students of Pareto's psychological sociology will realize how wise was this attitude of Brazilian leaders in the days of political liberalism. A sort of political fatigue seems to descend sometimes on the people vis-à-vis their leaders, like industrial fatigue among workers; and, according to a specialist in the human problems of an industrial civilization, Professor Elton Mayo (to whose ideas and work I have recently had the pleasure of being introduced by one of his former students), a scientific investigation of industrial fatigue suggests that merely listening to workers' complaints, even without acting on them, lessens the workers' fatigue and so increases their efficiency. There may be something of the same situation among politically-conscious people with regard to their leaders, who—if that is true—make a mistake when they try to suppress literary or popular criticism, satire, and caricature directed at their acts and personalities. King John VI of Brazil was ridiculed by many because he ate too much and sometimes carried fried chickens in his pockets; but he seems to have tolerated the true as well as the false stories circulated about him. The same tradition was followed by his grandson, the Emperor Dom Pedro II, who was freely criticized and caricatured in the Brazilian press on account of his devotion to astronomy and Hebrew, when so many popular needs and social problems went neglected; on account also of his almost feminine suavity when problems pressed whose solution, some of his critics thought, demanded the iron hand. As I have mentioned, Dom Pedro was called "Pedro Banana"—a nickname generally attached by Brazilians to people who are soft and lazy, but one that, applied seriously, was and is (as even foreigners have found out) a gross insult. Among the presidents of the Republic, a marshal of the Brazilian army, Hermes da Fonseca, was given the nickname of Dudú, and during his four years as president a number of articles and cartoons appeared in the press making fun of him and of his alleged power to spread bad luck. All three—King John VI, Emperor Dom Pedro II, and President Hermes da Fonseca—have become, if not national heroes, at any rate well-loved characters whom Brazilians regard with esteem and even affection. Even Senhor Washington Luis, when president of the Republic, though known as "Strong Arm," let himself be caricatured in *revistas* as a good eater and an old bohemian, and he was the butt of much satire and many caustic remarks in the daily press.

Such is the atmosphere in which Brazilian literature and painting have developed into an expression of social criticism and sometimes of social revolt. Both José Lins do Rego and Jorge Amado are master caricaturists, not photographic realists; their novels remind one of the Aleijadinho sculptures, of Gregorio de Mattos' satirical poetry, and of Euclydes da Cunha's *Os Sertões* [2] in that, though keenly alive to reality, each of these two most famous novelists of modern Brazil is a mixture of the artist and of the social critic; each is a poet in prose; each, though possibly deficient in sophisticated humour, is a powerful master of caricature and satire of the kind that simple men can understand. Sometimes José Lins do Rego—a sort of Brazilian William Falkner—writes as if he were copying from life; and he has copied from life to such a degree that some of his pages are rather those

---

2. This book has been recently translated into English by Mr. Samuel Putnam under the title *Revolt in the Backlands* and published by the University of Chicago Press, 1944.

from some vivid and powerful memoirs than those of a pure novelist. But he has a tendency to distort or exaggerate some of his characters so as to give them a symbolical value; one of these, Vitorino Carneiro da Cunha, has been acclaimed by critics who know Brazil well as a sort of Don Quixote of the sugar-cane plantations of Parahiba—a symbol, not a mere character.

The same thing has been accomplished by Jorge Amado in some of his best novels; in them he has adapted to literature part of the technique of the "A B C" or story-songs, through which news is propagated and men exalted or insulted among the masses of illiterate and semi-illiterate peasants of Brazil. His Balduino is a hero—the symbol of Negro vitality in Brazil. In this connection it is interesting to note that the name Balduino does not belong to the Christian calendar, from which so many Brazilians take the names they give their children; if I am not mistaken, its origin is popular and, at the same time, Anglo-American—it is a corruption of *Baldwin*, from the Baldwin locomotive! When Brazilian peasants talk of some powerful machine they call it a *Balduina;* and Jorge Amado's Negro hero seems to have something in him of the locomotive so admired by peasants and small boys, in that he is a human power, the symbol of the people's vitality, Afro-Brazilian vitality.

Of the modern Brazilian novelists who deal with social problems—authors like Lins do Rego, Jorge Amado, Raquel de Queiroz, Amando Fontes, Vianna Moog, and Erico Verissimo—one may say that, though realists, they are also romanticists, with a romantic yearning not so much for an imaginary past as for an imaginary future. Some of them come from the oldest and most feudal regions of Brazil—Pernambuco, Bahia, the North-east. And at least one, José Lins do Rego, is connected with an old but now decadent family of feudal Brazil. Nevertheless they are doing more than economists, more than politicians, more than demagogues to carry not only Brazilian literature, but the Brazilians themselves, away from an excess of colonial tradition in their behaviour and from oppressive colonial complexes of inferiority to Europe. In literature such excesses have meant the writing of novels, poetry, and essays in strictly academic Portuguese language and according to academic prescriptions and rigid European techniques, with the result that the literature has failed to express or interpret Brazilian reality.

As a consequence of their revolt against conventional techniques, their criticism of Brazilian life, and particularly their frankness in regard to sex and to the relations between whites and blacks and between rich and poor, the young Brazilian novelists have encountered opposition. They have come into conflict with the optimism of some Latin as well as Anglo-Americans who seek to give outsiders and themselves the impression that everything is well with young America, that nothing is wrong in Brazilian life; they have encountered the theory that literature should be an instrument of propaganda for the good and pleasant in that life, that it should avoid mockery, satire, or criticism of the sort that might convey the idea that Brazil has many Negroes and that it also has serious problems of maladjustment, poverty, and misery.

The same thing has happened to some of the modern Brazilian poets, historians, essayists, literary critics, and painters who are taking Brazilian culture and the mind of young Brazil out of that passively colonial and rigidly academic tradition in which there was no place for a literature or an art different from Europe's. This tradition made Brazilians afraid to express themselves freely. They were afraid to reveal how different Brazil was and is from Europe—a Europe considered socially and intellectually perfect by many Latin Americans with a colonial psychological complex of inferiority.

Some years ago a novel was published in Rio that may be regarded, in some of its aspects, as an anticipation of the modern social novel of Brazil. I refer to *Canaan*, written by Graça Aranha, an aristocrat descended from an old family of northern Brazil. Its plot has been summarized by the famous Italian historian and critic, Signor Guglielmo Ferrero, who says that its real subject is "the encounter of the races, the mixing of cultures, the disturbance caused in the social organization of all American countries by the masses of men arriving from overcrowded Europe." [3] But I think that *Canaan* is also the drama of Brazilians under the pressure of that old

---

3. Guglielmo Ferrero, "Preface," *Canaan*, by Graça Aranha; trans. from the Portuguese by Mariano Joaquin Lorente (Boston, 1920), p. 7.

colonial complex from which only now their historians, essayists, novelists, poets, and critics are vigorously liberating them.

One of the most significant characters in *Canaan* is Paulo Maciel, a young Brazilian lawyer. The way that he talks throughout the novel is the way that many Brazilian lawyers, intellectuals, and artists talked thirty or forty years ago, when they felt that Brazil was nothing more than "a colony of Europe." They saw no hope that Brazilians might overcome their colonial condition. At that time men like Paulo Maciel, though conscious of the dependence of Brazil upon Europe, did nothing to counteract it. When one of these men made a speech or wrote an article or a dissertation, a book or a poem, he wrote as though he expected to have to submit his grammar, composition, style, vocabulary, and ideas to a committee of Portuguese professors of grammar and to a committee of French professors of literature, law, or sociology from Paris. Nearly all of these men derived their ideas about Brazil, not from direct study of conditions, but from what remote and sometimes ignorant or second-rate French sociologists like Le Bon wrote about race mixture in Latin America. The best of the writers followed such European social theorists as Spencer and Comte, ignorant of extra-European conditions and problems. Consequently their attitude toward Brazil was one of pessimism, though very few dared to express themselves in public in such a way as to conflict with Brazilian official philosophy—the philosophy of those in power, an emphatic and superficial optimism as long as those who expressed it remained in power.

The following words are spoken by Paulo Maciel, the character in *Canaan* to whom I have referred, as he talks to some Brazilian colleagues: "You gentlemen speak of independence, but I don't see it. Brazil is, and has always been, a colony. Our regime is not a free one. We are a protectorate. . . . Tell me: where is our financial independence? What is the real money that dominates us? Where is our gold? What is the use of our miserable paper currency if it isn't to buy English pounds? Where is our public property? What little we have is mortgaged. The customs revenues are in the hands of the English. We have no ships. We have no railroads, either; they are all in the hands of the foreigners. Is it, or is it not, a colonial regime disguised with the name of free nation? Listen. You don't believe me. I would like to be able to preserve our moral and intellectual patrimony, our language, but rather than continue this poverty, this torpitude at which we have arrived, it is better for one of Rothschilds' bookkeepers to manage our financial affairs and for a German colonel to set things in order." [4] And later, speaking not to a fellow countryman but to a German, Milkau, to whom Brazil was "Canaan" and Europe the reverse of "Canaan," young Maciel in a still more pessimistic mood says: "My only wish is to get out of here, to exile myself, to leave the country and go with my people [fam-

4. *Canaan*, pp. 196–197.

ily] to live in some corner of Europe. . . . Europe! . . . Europe! . . . Yes, at least until the crisis is over." [5]

All this was typical of the psychological attitude of Brazilian intellectual youth forty and even thirty years ago. In contrast to a strictly official optimism, there was a Russian pessimism among writers, lawyers, and students, due to the impact of a deep complex of colonialism upon their minds and their entire personalities. For most of them Europe—Paris, or London, or Berlin—was the ideal place of escape, actual or imagined, from Brazilian colonialism. For some did take imaginary refuge—even the old historian and critic João Ribeiro did—by living intellectually in Europe; that is, by being *in* Brazil but not *of* it, attaching themselves mentally to Europe—to France, particularly—as colonials, as exiles.

It is curious that in Graça Aranha's novel the best explanation of Brazil's critical condition, as felt by her intellectuals, is given not by one of the Brazilian characters, but by the German, Milkau, whom the author represents as a European with a philosophical turn of mind. It is he who tells the typically pessimistic Brazilian intellectual of the early nineteen-hundreds that Brazil, having originated as a conglomeration of races and castes, masters and slaves, had created through master-and-slave contact an intermediate race of mestizos that was really the link between classes, the national tie. Their numbers increasing every day, these mestizos were appropriating the best positions. When the army

5. *Ibid.*, p. 293.

Modern Literature 171

(very important to a German as to a Latin American) had ceased to be "the appanage of the white man" and began to be taken over by the mestizos, a social revolution had started—"a revenge of the oppressed."

This generalization was only partly true, since, as I have pointed out, most of the mixed-bloods who became prominent in early Republican Brazil had done little more than take the places and carry on the leadership of the monarchist leaders, some of whom were already men of Negro blood.

But, according to Aranha's Milkau, whatever shock of conflict there was between the white and the heterogeneous leadership as a result of the Republican Revolution was "absolutely necessary to bring about what other means had not been able to accomplish for centuries: the formation of a nationality." [6]

This again is a generalization only partly true, for after their successful struggle against the Dutch in the seventeenth century some Brazilians began to feel and even to act as if they were capable of being a nationality. And since that early war for independence, leadership has been heterogeneous as far as military action was concerned. The four great heroes of the Brazilian war against the Dutch belonged to different races: one was a Portuguese, another was a white Brazilian, the third was an Indian, the fourth was a Negro. It was during the war against the Dutch that various men of African blood or modest social situation distinguished themselves by acts of bravery or by valiant services in

6. *Ibid.*, p. 295.

the defence of Brazil. These services were recognized, and they contributed to the social elevation of the men and in some cases to their entrance by marriage into the ranks of the highest Brazilian society. It was also during the war against the Dutch that Father Vieira—born in Portugal but educated in Brazil, where he arrived as a child—distinguished himself as an intellectual leader whose sermons and writings have not only a religious interest and a literary value but a deep psychological and sociological significance as a sort of manifesto—an ethnically democratic manifesto—against the idea of superiority of men over men based upon skin-colour. If this idea were true, he said once, the Dutch would have to be considered a superior race that could not be defeated by the Portuguese and the Brazilians; but it could not be true, since the Dutch were Protestant heretics and the Portuguese and the Brazilians were orthodox Catholics. Vieira thus made anthropology dependent upon theology and Catholic orthodoxy.

Though his father had been made a nobleman by the King of Portugal, Vieira was the grandson of a mulatto woman. When he preached race equality, he spoke *pro domo sua*. He was in a logical position to be the psychological and intellectual link in a social revolution that began in Brazil, not with the Republic in 1889, but during the wars against the Dutch in the seventeenth century: a revolution looking towards the admittance of mixed-bloods to leadership in Brazil, and towards the formation of a Brazilian nationality through an at first vague, and only today clear, consciousness or feeling of ethnic as well as social difference from Europe. But difference—not inferiority.

All this seems to have been forgotten by Graça Aranha's German philosopher on Brazilian history, Milkau, when he tells Maciel that the revolution against Europe in Brazil had begun with the Republic: with the 1889 victory of the Republican leaders who were army officers—some of them, as we know, men with Indian and Negro blood. But in the dialogue between Maciel and Milkau it is the Brazilian who is the Aryanist or Racist, the German who is the believer in the advantages of race mixture. It is the German (copied from life and not a purely literary invention) who tells the pessimistic Brazilian intellectual (representing the feeling of some of the best Brazilian intellectuals of one and two generations ago, including Euclydes da Cunha, Sylvio Romero, and Graça Aranha himself) that "there are no races capable or incapable of civilization" since "history is nothing but a record of the fusion of races." And, Milkau continues, "in Brazil, you may be sure, culture will flourish in the soil of the half-caste population because there has been there that divine fusion which is the creative force." In "a remote future, the period of the mulattoes will have passed," to be succeeded by "the period of the white people." The "white people . . . will accept the patrimony of their half-caste predecessors, who will have built something, for nothing passes uselessly over the earth." [7] As to Europe: "That Europe towards which you people turn your

7. *Ibid.*, p. 296.

longing and dying eyes and which you love with your tired souls, hungry for happiness, culture, art, and life, that Europe also suffers from the malady which disintegrates and kills. Do not allow yourselves to be dazzled by her empty pomp, by the useless strength of her armies, by the brilliance of her genius." [8]

I repeat that two contradictory views or philosophies of life and of Brazilian history were powerfully reflected in Brazilian literature until, soon after the First World War, new voices began to be heard, first from São Paulo, and then from the North-east. Of the two traditional views, one expressed an almost absolute optimism concerning Brazilian past, present, and future, and particularly the Amerindian basis of its "race" and "ethos." The extreme expression of this philosophy is to be found in a book entitled *Porque me ufano do meu paiz* ("Why I Am Proud of My Fatherland"), written by Afonso Celso, a good and distinguished, though naïve, Brazilian who was given the title of Count by the Holy See. The other philosophy combined an almost suicidal pessimism over Brazilian ethnic and social conditions with a longing for Europe, viewed with a sort of filial veneration as if London and Paris, Lisbon and Berlin each had a pope whom the Brazilians must follow blindly when studying law or sociology and writing poems or novels. Between the two extremes there had appeared a few books like *Os Sertões* by Euclydes da Cunha and *Canaan* by Graça Aranha, and some of the best pages of social and literary critics like

8. *Ibid.*, p. 297.

José Verissimo, Sylvio Romero, and Alberto Torres—and these were the harbingers of a new phase in Brazilian literature: the modern phase.

In 1919 a book was published in São Paulo, *Urupés*, which, though pessimistic rather than optimistic in its views of social conditions, nevertheless was far from colonial, academic, sub-European or orthodox *à la française* in style, in form, or language; it was vigorously Brazilian, full of native idioms, and marked by departures from rigid grammatical rules. Its author was Monteiro Lobato. *Urupés* is a collection of tales about the poor or decadent populations of rural Brazil, generally neglected by politicians and by conventional *literati* (though Euclydes da Cunha's *Os Sertões* had been a powerful pioneer study of central Brazil as a dramatic subject not only for literature but for sociology, anthropology, and human geography). The personality of the author of *Urupés*—even more than his first book or any that followed it—was to be a centre of intellectual and cultural revolution in Brazil. Dynamic, suggestive, stimulating, Lobato became a literary and social critic and creative artist, as well as a publisher. For years he published essays, novels, poems, sociological and historical studies written by promising young writers, the best of whom exhibited vigorous intellectual honesty and realism in dealing with Brazilian subjects and followed Lobato in his courageous use of native idioms and even in his disdain of Europe as Brazil's intellectual and cultural master.

In São Paulo and later in Rio, there followed another

literary revolution, significant as an attempt to express the Brazilian ethos and, to a certain extent, to reflect extra-European social and ethnic conditions. I refer to the movement called "Modernism" in Brazil. One of its most interesting leaders, Mario de Andrade, has recently regretted that it remained too exclusively a literary or narrowly artistic revolution, that it did not go far enough in developing its social implications. But there is no doubt that Brazilian "Modernism" did much to bring Brazilians to an awareness of their country. Fearless of the unapproved, in its reaction against academic artificiality "Modernism" sometimes became artificial itself. But it opened the door to a new Brazilian way of writing that has influenced and is still influencing the Portuguese written in Portugal.

Indepeñdently of the "Modernism" of Rio and São Paulo, a similar movement started in the oldest region of Brazil, the North-east. This also was a revolt against narrow colonialism, though it did not repudiate Brazilian experience and the integration of European with extra-European values during the colonial era. It proclaimed the need of extra-European attitudes and values, without failing to recognize the need in Brazil of a close contact with Europe and with its European past; Brazil should select from its colonial heritage a series of values that are in harmony with the tropical landscape and with Brazilian conditions of life. Hence the importance attached by some of its leaders to traditional cookery and pastry, traditional architecture, furniture, and popular art—not to preserve them as sacred things but to use them as honest beginnings for a really Brazilian art and way of living. Not a single or exclusive tradition—that of Aryan Europe—but a combination of traditional values: from the Arabs and Moors, from the Jews, from Africa, from Asia, should be followed, having as their basis the experience of the Portuguese and the heritage of the Amerindian.

Opposing the reaction against this combination, which had taken place during the nineteenth century when sophisticated Brazilians began to be ashamed of some of their best extra-European values and traditions, the leaders of the North-east movement argued that Brazil ought to maintain and develop the extra-European values and traditions already harmonized with tropical and Brazilian conditions of life, instead of neglecting or abandoning them in order to become a cultural province of Europe or of the United States. Impelled by this idea, the Congress of Regionalism met in 1925 in Recife, intellectual capital of the North-east, with Odilon Nestor, José Lins do Rego, Morais Coutinho, Annibal Fernandes, Luis Cedro, Julio Bello, and others as its leaders or followers. It was the first Congress of Regionalism in Brazil. Its manifesto was literary and artistic, but also sociological and political. Variety in unity characterized the proceedings, not only in the basic ideas of the program itself but also in the personnel, which included men of various ages and generations, temperaments and professions. It is safe to say that the group that met for this Congress—some of them still students or very recent graduates from universities—and those who since have been directly or indirectly influenced by them have produced some of modern Brazil's most interesting and vitally significant literature and social and literary criticism.

Resisting the idea that material or technical progress should be taken as the measure of Brazilian greatness, the regionalists stand for that love of locality that with them seems to be a pre-requisite for honest, authentic, genuine creative work—not an end in itself. These are no narrow nationalists; they realize that interdependence is, throughout the world, an essential condition for a more humane and more co-operative intellectual and artistic life. Some of their critics have accused them of being reactionaries; others have called them "Communists" or "Anarchists" who refuse to acknowledge the need for centralization, for rigid uniformity, in a country like Brazil. The truth is that the work already done by many of the most creative of them—José Lins do Rego, José Americo, Cicero Dias, Luis Jardim, Mario Marroquim, Alvaro Lins, Jorge de Lima, Odorico Tavares, Aurelio Buarque de Holanda, Julio Bello, Olivio Montenegro, Annibal Fernandes, E. Pinto, Luis Viana, Silvio Rabello—is vigorously constructive: it has done much to generate real unity and inter-regional understanding as well as to make Brazil a vital part of a new and more co-operative world.

The same might be said of the cultural revolution effected with a more immediate literary and artistic success by the "Modernists" of Rio and São Paulo—Mario de Andrade, Oswald de Andrade, Graça Aranha,

Alcantara Machado, Manuel Bandeira, Sergio Buarque, Prudente de Morais Neto, Ribeiro Conto, and others—whose movement at once initiated a new era in the intellectual and artistic development of Brazil.

These two movements will probably stand as the most significant in revolutionizing the letters and the life of Brazil in the direction of intellectual or cultural spontaneity, creativeness, and self-confidence set against the tradition of colonial subordination to Europe or the United States.

INDEX

Abend, Hallett, 127 n
Treaty Ports, 127 n
Albuquerque (Cavalcanti de) family, 13
Albuquerque, Jeronymo de, 28
Aleijadinho, 155-6, 157, 160, 161, 164
Alencar, José de, 116
Allen, Charles H., 110
letter in *The Anti-Slavery Reporter*, 110
Allston, Robert F. W., 64
Almeida, Alvaro Ozorio de, 100
Amado, Jorge, 158, 164, 165
Amaro, João, 44
American Language, The (Mencken), 33
American Negro Slavery (Phillips), 65 n
American Political Science Review, The, 69 n
American Revolution, 144
Americo, José, 178
Andrade, Carlos Drumond de, 85, 158
Andrade, Mario de, 176, 178
Andrade, Oswald de, 178
Anti-Slavery Reporter, The, 110
Arabs, 5-6
Arcoverde, Cardinal, 115
"*Aspectos de um seculo de transição*" (Freyre), 98 n
Azevedo, João Lucio de, 14, 18
Epocas de Portugal Economico, 14 n

Baker, Joseph E., 67
"Regionalism: Pro and Con. Four Arguments for Regionalism," 68 n
Bandeira, Manuel, 158, 179
Bates, Henry, 94, 133
Naturalist on the River Amazon, The, 94 n
Beals, Carleton, 128
"Soviet Wooing of Latin America, The," 129 n
Bell, Aubrey F. G., 8, 24
Portugal of the Portuguese, 8 n, 24 n
Bello, Julio de Albuquerque, 177, 178
Bews, J. W., 68
Human Ecology, 68 n
Bilden, Rüdiger, 133
Bingham, Hiram, 131
Monroe Doctrine, The, 131 n
Boas, Franz, 43
Bonifacio, José, 27, 118-19, 121
Bonn, Moritz Julius, 68
Brazil and La Plata: The Personal Record of a Cruise (Stewart), 125 n
Brazil and the Brazilians (Fletcher and Kidder), 134, 135 n
Brazil, A Study of Economic Types (Normano), 42 n, 78 n, 141
Brazil: Today and Tomorrow (Elliott), 45 n, 111 n, 114 n
"Brazil Under the Monarchy" (Creary), 47 n

Index

Brazil, Vital, 100
Brazilian Federal Department for the Protection of the Indians, 118
"Brazil's Foreign Policy" (Oliveira Lima), 145 n
British Foreign and State Papers; Reports from Committees, 48 n
Bryce, James, 98, 137–8
South America, Observations and Impressions, 98 n, 138 n
Buarque, Sergio, see Hollanda, Sergio Buarque de
Bureau of Indian Affairs (United States), 132
Bureau of Intercultural Education (United States), 132
Burton, Sir Richard Francis, 97
Highlands of Brazil, The, 97 n

Camara, Lima, 120
Camoëns, Luis de, 44
Canaam (Graça Aranha), 167–8, 169–71, 173 n, 174
Carneiro, Gomes, 118
Carneiro da Cunha, Vitorino, 165
Cedro, Luis, 177
Celso, Afonso, 174
Porque me ufano do meu paiz, 174
Chagas (scientist), 100
China and Europe (Reischwein), 31 n
"Chronicas Lageanas" (Creary), 47 n
Clark, Hamlet, 47
Letters Home from Spain, Algeria and Brazil, 48 n
Cleveland, Grover, 114
Cliff, José, 48

Climate of Portugal, The (Dalgado), 10 n
Clough, Shepard Bancroft (and Cole), 31 n
Economic History of Europe, 31 n
Coelho Pereira, Brites, 13
Coelho Pereira, Duarte, 13
Cole, Charles Woolsey (and Clough), 31 n
Economic History of Europe, 31 n
Colton, Walter, 134
Deck and Port, 134 n
Columbia University (New York), 49
"Comparison of the Effects of Certain Socioeconomic Factors upon Size of Family in China, Southern California, and Brazil, A" (Griffing), 61 n
Comte, Auguste, 103, 168
Concerning Latin American Culture, 4 n
Congress of Regionalism in Brazil (Recife), 66, 177
Conquest of Brazil, The (Nash), 20, 45 n, 135 n
Continho, Afranio, 66 n
"Some Considerations on the Problem of Philosophy in Brazil," 66 n
Conto, Ribeiro, 85, 179
Cotteril, R. S., 55
Old South, The, 55 n
Council Against Intolerance in America, 131–2
Council of Immigration and Colonization of Brazil, 120
Council on Intercultural Relations, 132

INDEX

Coutinho, Morais, 177
Creary, R., 46–7
  "Brazil Under the Monarchy," 47 n
  "Chronicas Lageanas," 47 n
Cruz, Oswaldo, 100
  Culto da Arte em Portugal, O (Ortigao), 31 n
Cunha, Euclydes da, 164, 173, 174, 175
  Sertões, Os, 164, 174, 175

Dalgado, D. G., 10
  Climate of Portugal, The, 10 n
Dampier, Sir William Cecil Dampier, and Catherine Durning, 43
  Family and the Nation, The 43
Dantas, Julio, 143
Deck and Port (Colton), 134 n
Dewey, John, 73
Dias, Cicero, 65, 157, 178
Díaz, Porfirio, 133
Dickens, Charles, 47
  Oliver Twist, 47
Dixon, Roland B., 43
  Documentary History of American Industrial Society (Phillips), 40 n

Economic History of Europe (Clough and Cole), 31 n
Elliott, L. E., 45, 111 n, 113, 114 n, 120
  Brazil: Today and Tomorrow, 45 n, 111 n, 114 n
Encyclopedia of the Social Sciences, 106, 126, 149 n
Epocas de Portugal Economico (Azevedo), 14 n

Ewbank, Thomas, 95–6, 97, 161
  Life in Brazil, or The Land of the Cocoa and the Palm, 96 n, 97 n, 161 n

Fair Employment Practices Committee (United States), 132
Falkner, William, 164
Family and the Nation, The (Dampier), 43
Federal Council of Churches of Christ in America, 132
Federal Farm Board (United States), 106
Fernandes, Annibal, 177, 178
Fernando, King of Portugal, 15, 16, 17
Ferrero, Guglielmo, 167 n
First World War, 130, 173
Fischer, Eugen, 10
Fletcher, J. C. (and Kidder), 134
  Brazil and the Brazilians, 134
Fonseca, Hermes da, 163–4
Fontes (scientist), 100
Fontes, Amando, 165
Franco, Francisco, 129
Frank, Waldo, 83, 89
  South American Journey, 89 n
French Revolution, 129
Freyre, Gilberto, 31 n, 46 n, 58 n, 98 n
  "Aspectos de um seculo de transição," 98 n
  Mundo que o Portugues Creou, O, 31 n
  "Social Life in the Middle of the 19th Century," 46 n, 58 n
Frontin, Paulo, 104

Index

Gaines, Francis Pendleton, 55, 56, 57
Southern Plantation, The, 55
Gamio, Manuel, 43
Ganivet, Ángel, 2
Genetic and Endocrine Basis for Differences in Form and Behavior, The (Stockard), 99 n
Giddings, Franklin, 72
Gillespie, James Edward, 31 n
Influence of Overseas Expansion on England (1500-1700), The, 31 n
Glicerio, Francisco, 103
Gobineau, Joseph Arthur, Count de, 133
Goetz, Walter, 149
"Jesuits," 149 n
Graça Aranha, José Pereira da, 167, 170-1, 173, 174, 178
Canaan, 167-8, 169-71, 173 n, 174
Granville, Granville George Leveson-Gower, Earl, 110
Greco, El (Domenico Theotocopuli), 157, 158
Griffing, John B., 61 n
"Comparison of the Effects of Certain Socioeconomic Factors upon Size of Family in China, Southern California, and Brazil, A," 61 n
"Natural Eugenics in Brazil," 61 n
Guenther, Konrad, 91, 92, 116, 133
Naturalist in Brazil, A, 91 n, 116 n

Hanke, Lewis, 154
Harper's Magazine, 129
Harvard University, 42
Hayes, Carlton, 49
Highlands of Brazil, The (Burton), 97 n
Hispanic American Historical Review, The, 46 n
History of Brazil (Southey), 49 n
Hollanda, Aurelio Buarque de, 178
Hollanda, Sergio Buarque de, 179
Hood, Thomas, 47
"Song of the Shirt, The," 47
Hooton, Earnest A., 42, 43
House, Edward Mandell, 127
Human Ecology (Bews), 68 n

Ihering, Rudolf von, 92
Imperial Academy of Medicine (Brazil), 60
Indians in Brazil, 114-20
Industrial Revolution, 49, 69
Influence of Overseas Expansion on England (1500-1700), The (Gillespie), 31 n
Inquisition, 7-8
Inter-American Conference of Philosophy, 66

Jardim, Luis, 178
Jefferson, Thomas, 129, 145
Jesuits, 7-8, 27, 28, 37, 39, 43-4, 87, 117, 118, 149
"Jesuits" (Goetz), 149 n
Jews, 5, 6, 8-10, 12, 13-14, 16-18, 25
John (João) VI, King of Brazil, 163, 164
Journal of Heredity, 61 n

Index

Keyserling, Hermann, Count, 98 n
Kidder, D. P. (and Fletcher), 134
Brazil and the Brazilians, 134, 135 n
Kohl, Johann Georg, 10
Kohn, Hans, 2 n, 125-6
Orient and Occident, 2 n, 126 n
"Race Conflict," 126 n
Koster, Henry, 48
Travels in Brazil, 49 n

Las Casas, Bartolomé de, 27
League of Nations Covenant, 127
Le Bon, Gustave, 168
Legendre, Maurice, 2
Portrait de l'Espagne, 2 n
legends, Portuguese, 20-3
Lentz, Fritz, 132, 133
Letters Home from Spain, Algeria and Brazil (Clark), 48 n
Lewinson, Paul, 126 n
Race, Class and Party, 126 n
Library of Congress, 47
Life in Brazil, or The Land of the Cocoa and the Palm (Ewbank), 96 n, 97 n, 161 n
Lima, Jorge de, 158, 178
Lima, Manoel de Oliveira, 145
"Brazil's Foreign Policy," 145 n
Lins, Alvaro, 178
Lins, Sinval, 100
Lins do Rego, José, 65, 158, 164, 165, 166, 177, 178
Livro do Nordeste, 98 n
Lobato, Monteiro, 175
Urupés, 175

London Labour and the London Poor (Mayhew), 47
Lorente, Mariano Joaquin, 167 n
Luis, Washington, 164

Machado, Alcantara, 45, 178
Machado, Pinheiro, 52
Magalhães, Basilio de, 45
Maia, José Joaquim da, 145
Mann, Thomas, 64
Marinho, Joaquim Saldanha, 79
Marroquim, Mario, 178
Martius, Karl Friedrich Philipp, von, 133
Mattos, Gregorio de, 159-60, 161, 164
Maura, Bishop of, 130
Mayhew, Henry, 47
London Labour and the London Poor, 47
Mayo, Elton, 163
Meade, Richard Kidder, 146
Mello, Silva, 100
Memoria sobre a população e a agricultura de Portugal desde a fundação da monarchia até 1865 (L. S. Rebello da Silva), 11 n
Mencken, H. L., 33
American Language, The, 33
Mendes, Murilo, 158
Miall, Bernard, 91 n
Monroe Doctrine, The (Bingham), 131 n
Montenegro, Olivio, 178
Moog, Vianna, 165
Moors, 5, 6, 19-22
Morais, Venicius de, 158
Morais Neto, Prudente de, 179
Moreira, Juliano, 147
Moreira de Barros, 108
Morrow, Glenn R., 66

Moscow Conference, 128
Müller, Lauro, 104, 153
Mundo que o Portugues Creou, O (Freyre), 31 *n*
Murphy, James, 22
  Travels in Portugal, 22 *n*

Nabuco, Joaquim, 53, 65
Narrative of a Voyage to the South Atlantic (Webster), 48 *n*, 51 *n*
Narrative of Travels on the Amazon and Rio Negro, A (Wallace), 47 *n*
Nash, Roy, 19–20, 45, 135
  Conquest of Brazil, The, 20, 45 *n*, 135 *n*
National Association for the Advancement of Colored People (United States), 132
National Conference of Christians and Jews, (United States), 132
National Maritime Union (United States), 132
"Native Policy" (Ots y Capdequi), 149 *n*
"Natural Eugenics in Brazil" (Griffing), 61 *n*
Naturalist in Brazil, A (Guenther), 91 *n*, 116 *n*
Naturalist on the River Amazon, The (Bates), 94 *n*
Nestor, Odilon, 177
New Viewpoints on the Spanish Colonization of America (Zavala), 26, 27 *n*
Normano, J. F., 42, 78 *n*, 141
  Brazil, A Study of Economic Types, 42 *n*, 78 *n*, 141
Notices of Brazil in 1828 and 1829 (Walsh), 70 *n*
Nuñez, Mendieta, 43

Old South, The (Cotteril), 55 *n*
Oliver Twist (Dickens), 47
Orient and Occident, 2 *n*
Orozco, José Clemente, 157
Ortigão, Ramalho, 31 *n*
  Culto da Arte em Portugal, O, 31 *n*
Ots y Capdequi, José, 149
  "Native Policy," 149 *n*
Oumansky, Constantin A., 128

Pará; or Scenes and Adventures on the Banks of the Amazon (Warren), 58 *n*
Paraná, Honorio Hermeto Carneiro Leão, Marquis of, 52–3
Pareto, Vilfredo, 162
Patronato Agricola, 112
Paulding, James K., 56
  Westward Ho!, 56
Peçanha, Nilo, 104, 153
Pedro II, Emperor of Brazil, 28, 53, 60, 97, 101, 109, 130, 134, 146, 163, 164
Pennsylvania, University of, 66
Pereira de Souza, Washington Luis, *see* Luis, Washington
Pessôa, Epitacio, 109
Pfeiffer, Ida, 47
  Voyage autour du Monde, 47 *n*
Philip II, King of Spain, 26, 39, 74, 90
Phillips, Ulrich B., 40, 57, 65
  American Negro Slavery, 65 *n*
  Documentary History of American Industrial Society, 40 *n*
  Plantation and Frontier, 1649–1863, 40 *n*
Pierson, Donald, 133

INDEX

Pinto Roquette, E., 43, 100, 135, 178
Plantation and Frontier (Phillips), 40 *n*
"Plantation: the Physical Basis of Traditional Race Relations, The," 55 *n*
Pombal, Sebastião José de Carvalho e Mello, Marquis of, 7
Porque me ufano do meu paiz (Celso), 174
Portinari, Candido, 157
Portrait de l'Espagne (Legendre), 2 *n*
Portugal of the Portuguese (Bell), 8 *n*, 24 *n*
Portuguese Pioneers, The (Prestage), 31 *n*
Potter, Pitman B., 69 *n*
"Universalism Versus Regionalism in International Reorganization," 69 *n*
Prado, Paulo, 45
Putnam, Samuel, 164 *n*
Prestage, Edgar, 31 *n*
Portuguese Pioneers, The, 31 *n*

Queiroz, Raquel de, 158, 165

Rabello, Silvio, 178
Race, Class and Party (Lewinson), 126 *n*
"Race Conflict" (Kohn), 126 *n*
Race Relations and the Race Problem (Thompson), 55 *n*
Radosavlevich, F. R., 133
Ramalho, João, 28
Rebello, L. S. Silva, 11 *n*
Memoria sobre a populaçao e a agricultura de Portugal desde a fundaçao da monarchia até 1865, 11 *n*
Rebouças, André, 79
regionalism in Brazil, 66–70
"Regionalism: Pro and Con. Four Arguments for Regionalism" (Baker), 68 *n*
Reischwein, Adolphe, 31 *n*
China and Euproe, 31 *n*
Reports from Committees (House of Commons), *Session of 1847-1848*, 48 *n*
Revolt in the Backlands, see *Sertões, Os*
Ribeiro, João, 45, 170
Ricardo, Antonio, 45
Ricardo, Cassiano, 45
Ríos, Fernando de los, 4
Rivera, Diego, 157
Romero, Sylvio, 65, 121, 173, 175
Rondon, see Silva Rondon
Roosevelt, Theodore, 33, 75, 136
Through the Brazilian Wilderness, 33 *n*, 137 *n*
Rosas, Juan Manuel de, 152

Saldanha Marinho, 79
Sampaio, Theodoro, 45
Sancho II, King of Portugal, 18
Sanderson, Dwight, 29
Santos, Constantino José dos, 15 *n*
São Paulo Congress, 81
Schulten, Adolf, 2
Select Committee on Coffee and Sugar Planting, 48
Sergio, Antonio, 14, 15 *n*
Sketch of the History of Portugal, A, 15 *n*
Sertões, Os (Cunha), 164, 174, 175

Index

Silva Rondon, Candido Mariano, 118, 120
Siqueira, Jacintha de, 96
Sketch of the History of Portugal, A (Sergio), 15 *n*
Sobieski (Polish traveller, *fl.* 1611), 8
"Social Life in the Middle of the 19th Century" (Freyre), 46 *n*, 58 *n*
Sombart, W., 16–17
"Some Considerations on the Problem of Philosophy in Brazil" (Continho), 66 *n*
"Song of the Shirt, The," (Hood), 47
South America, Observations and Impressions (Bryce), 98 *n*, 138 *n*
South American Journey (Frank), 89 *n*
Southern Plantation, The (Gaines), 55
Southey, Robert, 49
  History of Brazil, 49 *n*
"Soviet Wooing of Latin America, The" (Beals), 129 *n*
"Spain in the Epoch of American Civilization," 4 *n*
Spencer, Herbert, 168
Stewart, C. S., 124–5, 133
  Brazil and La Plata: The Personal Record of a Cruise, 125 *n*
Stockard, Charles R., 99
  Genetic and Endocrine Basis for Differences in Form and Behavior, The, 99 *n*
Study of War, A (Wright), 69 *n*

Taunay, Affonso de E., 45
Tavares, Odorico, 158, 178
Taylor, Robert Love, 54–5
Thompson, Edgar T., 55, 57
  Race Relations and the Race Problem, 55 *n*
Through the Brazilian Wilderness (Roosevelt), 33 *n*, 137 *n*
Tong King Sing, 108, 110
Torres, Alberto, 175
Travels in Brazil (Koster), 49 *n*
Travels in Portugal (Murphy), 22 *n*
Treaty Ports (Abend), 127 *n*
Turner, Frederick Jackson, 42, 67, 77

Ugarte, Manuel, 153
Unamuno, Miguel de, 2
"Universalism Versus Regionalism in International Reorganization" (Potter), 69 *n*
University of Chicago Press, 164
Urupés (Lobato), 175

"Valorization" (Whittlesey), 106
Vargas, Getulio, 78, 86, 87, 90
Veblen, Thorstein, 59
Velloso de Oliveira, Henrique, 139
Verissimo, Érico, 165
Verissimo, José, 175
Viana, Luis, 178
Vieira, Antonio, 172
Villa-Lobos, Heitor, 158
Voyage autour du Monde (Pfeiffer), 47 *n*

INDEX

Wallace, Alfred Russel, 47, 133
  Narrative of Travels on the Amazon and Rio Negro, A, 47 *n*
Walsh, R., 70 *n*
  Notices of Brazil in 1828 and 1829, 70 *n*
Warren, John Esaias, 58
  Pará; or Scenes and Adventures on the Banks of the Amazon, 58 *n*
Washington, George, 129
Webster, W. H. B., 48, 51
  Narrative of a Voyage to the South Atlantic, 48 *n*, 51 *n*
Westward Ho! (Paulding), 56
Whetham, William Cecil Dampier and Catherine Durning, *see* Dampier

Whittlesey, Charles R., 106
  "Valorization," 106
"Why I am Proud of My Fatherland," *see Porque me ufano do meu paiz*
Wilson, Woodrow, 127, 129
Wright, Quincy, 69 *n*
  Study of War, A, 69 *n*

Xavier, St. Francis, 31

Yale University, 66, 131

Zavala, Silvio, 26
  New Viewpoints on the Spanish Colonization of America, 26, 27 *n*
Zola, Emile, 87

A NOTE ON THE TYPE IN WHICH
THIS BOOK IS SET

This book was set on the Linotype in *Janson*, a recutting made direct from the type cast from matrices made by Anton Janson some time between 1660 and 1687.
Of Janson's origin nothing is known. He may have been a relative of Justus Janson, a printer of Danish birth who practised in Leipzig from 1614 to 1635. Some time between 1657 and 1668 Anton Janson, a punch-cutter and type-founder, bought from the Leipzig printer Johann Erich Hahn the type-foundry which had formerly been a part of the printing house of M. Friedrich Lankisch. Janson's types were first shown in a specimen sheet issued at Leipzig about 1675. Janson's successor, and perhaps his son-in-law, Johann Karl Edling, issued a specimen sheet of Janson types in 1689. His heirs sold the Janson matrices in Holland to Wolffgang Dietrich Erhardt, of Leipzig.
The book was composed, printed, and bound by H. Wolff, New York. Typography by James Hendrickson.

Lightning Source UK Ltd.
Milton Keynes UK
19 November 2009

146467UK00001B/65/A